What Leaders Are Saying about
Leveling the Praying Field

Here is the voice we need for today's modern movement of prayer! Donna Barrett's genuine love for the Church and passion for prayer shine through in this practical, engaging guide to putting prayer back in the hands—and on the lips!—of all God's people. *Leveling the Praying Field* is an accessible resource filled with wisdom for every believer. Donna's unassuming approach demystifies the practice of prayer in both corporate and personal settings, making room for every believer to participate in the simple spiritual lifeline that is talking to and hearing from God. *Leveling the Praying Field* is sure to become a key tool for spiritual leaders and communities to open the floodgates of communication between God and His people!

Dick Eastman
International President, Every Home for Christ
President, America's National Prayer Committee

In our superdistracting twenty-first century world, no spiritual discipline seems to be more easily neglected and underpracticed than prayer. In her new book *Leveling the Praying Field,* Donna Barrett calls believers to re-engage in practical prayer for everyday real life. She challenges the assumptions of those who would leave prayer to the "intercessors" or "prayer warriors," reminding all who love God of the great privilege of simply talking to and listening to Him. Barrett's particular focus on the relationship between prayer and the work and gifts of the Spirit is a valuable contribution for Pentecostals and will inspire all who hunger for a deeper life of prayer and intercession. *Leveling the Praying Field* is readable and warmly relatable from the author's own pastoral experiences. This is a welcome addition from a spiritual leader to spur God's people to the Jesus-called discipline of prayer.

Dr. Beth Grant
Missionary
Cofounder Project Rescue,
AG Executive Presbyter

Amidst all our distractions, God is calling His church corporately and His people personally back to the place of prayer. In her book, *Leveling the Praying Field,* Donna Barrett gives us a wonderful gift of perspective and instruction for the journey toward such a life of prayerfulness. I recommend it highly! Its ring of integrity comes from the credibility of her own prayer-filled life and faith-filled hunger for God.

Dr. James Bradford
Lead Pastor
Central Assembly of God, Springfield, MO
Former General Secretary
General Council of the Assemblies of God

Donna Barrett does a phenomenal job of leveling the praying field for all by rekindling a passion and purpose for prayer within the believer's heart. This book breathes new life on an age-old practice that sadly too many times becomes jaded or pushed to the side in the church. If you want to go deeper, pray bolder, and see greater in your life, church, and community, I encourage you to dive into the power of prayer by leveling the praying field with this life-giving resource. It will change the way you pray!

Dr. Melissa Alfaro
Copastor of El Tabernaculo AD
AG Under 40 Executive Presbyter

Donna's deep passion in prayer and longing to see others draw closer to Him in conversation is contagious. For over a decade I have seen the very practical principles in this book walked out in her life and ministry. She "walks what she talks" and helps others jump onboard.

Her rich legacy as founding pastor of Rockside Church includes the understanding that prayer is the most important work we can do. We continue to reap the benefits of doing nothing without asking our Heavenly Father for His wisdom and help.

If you want to grow in prayer and help others do the same, this book is pure gold.

Catherine Monnin
Missions/Outreach Director
Rockside Church

It's one thing to have the list of ingredients for a recipe. It's another to have the recipe prepared by skillful, experienced hands. I can't think of anyone whose years of personal skill and passion for prayer have better prepared them for such a milestone project as *Leveling the Praying Field*. Like everyone who is privileged to know Donna Barrett, I gladly stand up and testify she is a child of God and stellar leader who regards prayer as essential to life as the air we breathe.

John Wootton
District Superintendent
Ohio Ministry Network

Donna Barrett is a gifted leader with a passion for Jesus, unquestionable integrity, and a burden to call the body of Christ back to the place of prayer. I highly recommend her new book, *Leveling the Praying Field*. This book will help you develop a more vibrant prayer life.

Brian Alarid
President and CEO
America Prays

Prayer is access to God. When looking at the impossible through the lens of prayer, you will now see as God sees. The angel said to Mary in Luke 1:37 (KJV), "With God nothing shall be impossible."

The desire of the author is that through reading this book, the reader will become a person of prayer. God has promised to answer prayer, and in James 5:16 (KJV), it is states "the effectual fervent prayer of a righteous man avails much." Prayer brings God into our life and makes it possible for us to see miracles happen.

Rev. Thomas Trask
Former General Superintendent
General Council of the Assemblies of God

Jesus called us to abide in Him—in essence, a call to talk to Him often (John 15:5). Even the short prayers of weak and broken people move God's heart because of His grace. Too often, believers have relegated prayer to a special group, rather than recognizing it as a great privilege for all of us to walk in throughout each day. *Leveling the Praying Field* celebrates the wonderful access that each of us has to the Father because of the blood of Jesus. Donna Barrett helps to identify and remove the barriers that keep us from enjoying the Lord's presence in prayer. As you read this book, embrace the Spirit's call to greater intimacy with Jesus.

This book gives a practical snapshot of what prayer looks like lived out at the grassroots level even while engaged in full-time work and service. In the midst of the distractions of a busy life and ministry, there is a way to engage in prayer as a priority in our life. You'll read about practical ways that prayer and ministry flow together instead of seeing them as competing realities.

Mike Bickle
International House of Prayer of Kansas City

LEVELING THE
PRAYING
FIELD

*HELPING EVERY PERSON
TALK TO GOD AND
HEAR FROM GOD*

DONNA L. BARRETT

Gospel Publishing House

ISBN: 978-1-60731-594-0

02-7042

Printed in the United States of America

23 22 21 • 3 4 5

There's no greater gift a friend can give than to partner in prayer, to join you in talking to God and hearing from God. I've been blessed many times over with such friends—friends who prayed with me, prayed for me, and allowed me to peek over their shoulder to show me what prayer looks like through their lens and experience. For them I'm eternally grateful, and I dedicate this book to:

Lori Kowal Scopelite, Vaso Suhodolsky,
Pam Ecrement, Amber Helms,
Nancy Bukovnik, Cathy Monnin,
Bill and Harriet Mouer, and
my seven male colleagues
in our monthly "Peer Group"

Contents

Foreword

When some folks talk about prayer, it's easy to feel convicted about your own habits. With some people, though, just talking with them about prayer makes you feel motivated to engage.

Donna Barrett is that kind of person. You can tell that for her, prayer is a part of life, not just an occupational obligation.

Donna has always been known as a person of prayer, both in student ministries and as a church-planting pastor. She's always created a culture of prayer wherever she's been, considering it one of the most important aspects of life-giving ministry.

I met Donna Barrett when I was a district Youth director and she was a youth pastor in Youngstown, Ohio. The spiritual depth of that youth group was a result of her teaching her students the importance and the value of prayer, even at an early age.

The outgrowth of prayer has followed Donna everywhere, from not only the churches and community that she's led, but even here at the national office. Within the first year of her leadership, she introduced our employees to a prayer campaign in seeking God for the city, and I'm watching it produce supernatural results in the lives of people within our community.

When you have the opportunity to be in a prayer meeting with Donna, you never feel intimidated by her mature prayer life. You believe, "I can be this kind of intercessor, too." I've heard her say that the sign of a successful prayer time is when we've helped others to grow in their willingness to talk to God and to hear from God for themselves. And that really defines the prayer person of Donna Barrett.

Prayer is more than an orator performance—it's conversation. You have to listen at least as much as you speak. There are times a person can pray so loud that they can't hear what God wants to say to them. *Leveling the Praying Field* will show you how to place a high priority on the value of listening in prayer as much as talking.

As you read this book, I hope you'll feel motivation to pray more, rather than guilt for not praying enough; that you would see not the deficiency of your prayer life, but rather the capacity for your prayer life to grow; and that your prayer life sharpens and your discernment keenly improves, both for things you can see and the things you can't.

It's a delight for me to invite you to go on this journey with Donna Barrett and our Fellowship as we engage in a deeper conversation with the Lord.

Doug Clay
General Superintendent
General Council of the Assemblies of God

Introduction

Do you feel like prayer is important, but just not your "thing"? If you were totally honest, would you admit that you find prayer boring? Or perhaps you're not sure it makes a difference or is really the best use of your time. Perhaps you find prayer intimidating because you don't feel like you're good at it, don't know how to pray, how to use the "right words," or how to have the endurance to stay with it.

If you answered yes to any of those ideas, this book is for you. Too often prayer looks like an activity on a sports field. You know, a select group of athletes make up two teams who are in fantastic shape, well-practiced, and highly trained. They do their thing at such a level of expertise that the spectators in the stands are wowed and amazed! Though a fan may toss the ball around in their backyard, that person knows full well they can't play at the level of the pros down on the field. It's easy to develop a similar categorization of those who pray.

We don't call them "professionals," but you know who I'm talking about. They love to attend prayer meetings and never blink when someone asks them to pray. Their flowing words move the emotions of those who listen. We even find tags and titles for these people: we call them "prayer warriors" or "intercessors." But where does that leave the rest of us? Doesn't God want to hear from each one of us? Doesn't He want to speak to every person, not just a few representatives? Of course, He does!

You might even feel intimidated to pray because of people who are close and dear to you. After I spoke at a service one evening, a friendly gentleman waited until others had moved on before he spoke to me. He glanced around to be sure no one was within earshot and said softly but intensely, "What you shared tonight is exactly where I am regarding prayer: intimidated. I feel upstaged by my wife. Even though I serve on the church board and have been a Christian for years, when I married my wife,

I took a back seat in the prayer department. She prays far more than I do. Her words are eloquent and scriptural, and she prays long prayers effortlessly. When we got married, I just surrendered the family prayer area to her because I felt like she was the better 'pray-er.' What you said tonight made me realize that God wants to hear from me, and I need to find my own on-ramp in prayer."

Does that sound familiar? When it comes to prayer, we need to *level the praying field*, to peel back the professional status of the few that causes others to feel like spectators rather than participants. We need to help everyone get in on the action!

——————————

In my earliest memory of prayer, I was reciting a familiar rhyme from a cross-stitch that hung over my bed with phrases like "dying before I wake" and "the Lord my soul to take." It was neither comforting nor personal, but I prayed it.

My next memory, as an elementary-age child, was of going forward to an altar after a Sunday morning sermon at the church our family attended irregularly. I knelt at the altar and a stern, elderly lady quickly joined me.

She seemed to be on assignment as she insistently pumped for an answer to her question, "What do you want to pray about?" I really didn't know. I was just drawn toward God and wanted to talk to Him. After the third repeat of her request, I felt obligated to give an answer, so I asked for prayer for my uncle who was going through a divorce. She prayed for him, I listened to her pray, and then returned to my seat unsatisfied.

Looking back on that experience I now realize that I needed to pray for my sins to be forgiven and for Jesus to be my Lord and Savior. Prayer can be such a clumsy experience.

My next memory of a trip to an altar took place years later, on another Sunday morning at a different church (Highway Tabernacle Assembly of God in Youngstown, Ohio). By now I was fifteen, and this time I elbowed my sister, Brenda, who is two years older, to go forward with me. The pastor, Jay Alford, led several of us to repeat a prayer that would change my life. It included words something like, "Jesus, forgive me of my sins, come into my life, and be my Savior and Lord."

Prayer. How does one learn to pray? Sometimes we talk about it and post on Facebook "My prayers are with you" like we all have a common understanding of what it means. Often we don't have a clue. Following a disaster, news reporters will make a general request for prayers, assuming we all know how to pray, but do we?

There are plenty of books out there about prayer. So why this one? This book on prayer is the practical result of a lifetime of wrestling with the ups and downs and observations of prayer, first as a teenager and then a young adult following Jesus. Later, when I stepped into the role of a pastor, I needed to pray for myself and others, as well as lead others in praying. As a clergy member in the community, I was called to pray at all types of events, from the start of a car race that was part of a television show, to parades, city council meetings, funerals, and graduations.

These many years, I've felt a huge range of emotions around prayer—joy, frustration, satisfaction, and a little bit of disappointment. I felt *joy* at the early realization that the Creator of the universe was willing to—*wanted* to—hear from me and talk to me. Wow! I could hardly get my mind around that reality. If a staff meets with their CEO regularly for vision, direction, and leadership, imagine the privilege of having a "staff meeting" with the God of the universe—one-on-one time to talk about God's vision, direction, and desires for me. (He wants that for you, too!)

I've also felt *frustrated* at times, realizing I really didn't know how to pray or how to hear from God. It seemed more logical to turn in a prayer request to my pastor or listen to someone else pray. It's also frustrating to observe people involved in all types of church activities who aren't also involved in prayer. It seems to me that when Jesus sets the example in prayer, and the Bible is full of support and instructions and commands for prayer, then His followers should be people of prayer.

Since I began to connect with God in prayer, nothing has been more fulfilling in my life. Here's the humbling reality: It's satisfying for God, too. I love the scene in the movie *Pinocchio* when the woodcarver sees his finished work turn from a wooden puppet to a living boy. Of all God has created, His sons and daughters are His special delight. From Genesis to Revelation, God wants a family for Himself, and a healthy family has quality conversation. Imagine the satisfaction He experiences when His created-ones talk to Him and listen to Him.

If this book accomplishes what I hope it will, you'll find yourself better able to talk to God, hear from God, and help others do the same. This book is for everyone who would like to talk to God and hear from God without feeling intimidated, without sensing they've trespassed onto the private entitlement of a privileged few. It's also a book for those who would like to help others participate more freely in prayer.

Prayer is for all of us. Whether you're nine or ninety-nine, have a third-grade education or a PhD, are president of a corporation, a waiter, or a construction worker, are female or male, God wants to hear from you, and He wants to share His ideas with you. Simply put, it's time for every person to get out of the stands and onto the field. It's time to *level the praying field.*

1

Talking to God, Hearing from God

"Prayer is the highest order of business, for it links a powerless human to the creative force of God's sovereign power."

—Dick Eastman

In an honest conversation with Tom, an over-the-road truck driver, we were talking about prayer. He said to me, "Oh, I have plenty of time to pray. I'm just not sure how to pray. I'm behind the wheel of my rig for hours on end. I pray for God to forgive me, to keep me safe on the road, to bless and help all my family members by name, and I thank Him for my blessings.

By that time about three minutes have passed, and I don't know what else to say!"

Can you relate to that? In responding to my trucker friend, I explained that prayer is the communication tool in our relationship with God, so it's like talking to a friend. I encouraged him to envision Jesus sitting in the passenger's seat of the rig and having a conversation with Him about hopes and dreams, neighbors and nations. The idea would be for my friend to say a few lines to God, then listen to what God might want to say to him.

If you feel like you don't have a clue how to pray, you're in good company. The disciples of Jesus felt the same way. That's why they asked Him to teach them how to pray:

> **One day Jesus was praying in a certain place. When he finished, one of his disciples said to him, "Lord, teach us to pray, just as John taught his disciples"** (Luke 11:1).

This passage doesn't record the prayer Jesus had just finished praying. In fact, it doesn't tell us any detail except that He was praying in a certain place. Was He praying on His knees or standing with hands raised? We don't know. Was it a long prayer or a short prayer? The Bible doesn't say. Was Jesus praying in a whisper or a loud voice? We don't know. Was He crying out to God or smiling and laughing with God? The Bible doesn't record any of those details.

What we *do* know is that when He finished praying, the disciples who had overheard Him wanted to pray, too. There was something

> Growing in your prayer life is like developing a muscle. You must be intentional and have a plan.

about Jesus' prayer that caused His disciples to say, "We want to be able to talk to God and hear from God like that." They weren't satisfied just to listen to Jesus pray, they wanted in on it! They knew prayer wasn't a spectator activity. They wanted to be personally involved. They didn't want one or two of the Twelve to become specialists who did the praying for the group. They asked, "Teach *us*, all of us, how to pray."

So, Jesus provided a template for them to learn to pray. It's brief. You can recite it as is or use each phrase as a springboard to talk to God. In that moment, the Lord's prayer became the disciples' prayer as Jesus taught them:

> **"Our Father in heaven,**
> **Hallowed be Your name.**
> **Your kingdom come.**
> **Your will be done**
> **On earth as it is in heaven.**
> **Give us this day our daily bread.**
> **And forgive us our debts,**
> **As we forgive our debtors.**
> **And do not lead us into temptation,**
> **But deliver us from the evil one.**
> **For Yours is the kingdom and the power**
> **and the glory forever. Amen"**
> **(Matthew 6:9–13, NKJV).**

It's a short and simple prayer, but powerful. Note how the first five lines describe who we pray to: the King of the Universe, the one true God, our Heavenly Father whose will must be done in heaven and earth.

The second five lines describe why we pray: to ask for our daily needs, to ask for forgiveness of our sins, and to ask for God's guidance.

The last line closes the prayer with adoration and praise that acknowledges God's authority over our lives as His children.

Jesus taught His disciples how to pray by giving them a prayer-pattern that would help them create their own prayers. It's a good place to start—a launching pad to springboard you into a series of themes that are woven well together to know the Lord. You can recite the prayer word-for-word or use it as a starting point for your own conversations with God.

Intentional Prayer

Growing in your prayer life is like developing a muscle. You must be intentional to be effective in praying. Intentional prayer is made with a plan, a place, and a personal style.

A Plan to Pray

Intentional prayer begins with a plan. I often say you can tell what a person or church values by looking at two things: their calendar and their finances. So, look at your calendar for the last month of scheduled times for activities and appointments. We make appointments with clients, the life coach, the hairstylist, the dentist, and the mechanic. Why not write in appointments with Jesus for times of prayer?

"How relational is that?" you might ask. Well, the friends I want to keep in touch with are the ones with scheduled phone appointments on my calendar, whether they live nearby or across the miles. Without a specific appointment, my friends and I might play phone tag for weeks until we give up trying, then months go by and the relationship drifts. Consider scheduling times of prayer on your weekly and monthly calendars, and keep the appointments as diligently as any other appointment on your schedule.

Coaching for Pastors

When I pastored, most of my sermons included what my congregation fondly came to know as SMWILL: "Show me what it looks like." I consistently shared from my own life or illustrations from others practical examples of how to apply the message in the sermon. Can I show you what it looks like to schedule prayer opportunities into your calendar?

A valued habit I've had since becoming a Christian at age fifteen is to block off the first full week of the new year with nightly prayer gatherings at church. The Assemblies of God fellowship I work with hosts this Week of Prayer for every church with calendar reminders and resources urging everyone to begin their new year with a concentrated focus on prayer and fasting. These times of prayer have been important benchmarks in my life: when God spoke clearly about a relationship He wanted me to end and when a career change opened the door for vocational ministry and leaving the law office.

While pastoring, I set aside time each quarter for a personal out-of-town prayer focus, whether at a cabin in a retreat center, a trip to the International House of Prayer in Kansas City, time on the beach, or a trip to a friend's house where the focus would be on prayer and God's Word. This type of thing doesn't happen without advance planning to make reservations, block out dates, and recruit a travel buddy suitable for the purpose of the trip.

As a pastor, I scheduled weekly appointments to pray in the sanctuary of our church with other ministries.

I met monthly for two hours every third Monday of the month for three years with a group that led a ministry to human-trafficking participants.

We held a time for prayer that started forty-five minutes before service each Sunday to prepare our hearts for service.

We hosted "power-lunch breaks" with prayer in the sanctuary for anyone who wanted to drop by for prayer on their noon break.

We put careful planning into the church calendar for all types of activities, so why not include planned prayer? You'll be glad you did if you plan and prepare for your own personal times of prayer.

A Place to Pray

Thankfully we can pray anywhere, but there are places that will work better than others for you. The type of place isn't the same for everyone. You might need to switch it up from time to time, and there might be several places that are great for prayer where you just naturally connect well with God when you are in *that place.* For you, it could be in a deer stand at the crack of dawn, in your vehicle, in your garage, in your basement, or in a literal "prayer closet." You don't have to pray in the same place all the time, but designating *some* place and being tuned in to the types of places that work for you can help you connect well and often with God.

For me, the place has shifted over the years. I have a "prayer chair" with a reading lamp and a place for my journal, Bible, devotionals, and a cup of coffee.

That works for a daily habit. Other places I've found to work for me have been the sanctuary of whatever church I am attending at the time. When no one else is around, I love to kneel at an altar or find a pew or chair to "crash" at and be with God. Walking on the beach (which only happens a few times a year) seems to bring tears to my eyes, and God feels close to my heart. Anything outdoors, whether it's the metro parks, a chair on a back deck, a bike trail, retreat-center walking paths, or a late-night bonfire seems to awaken my spirit to the nearness of God.

> Spaces and places— they keep prayer interesting.

On the other end of the spectrum, it helps to keep in mind that some places are too distracting to connect well with God. You can spy out a place or two that works well for you and see if it doesn't make a difference.

I seem to have done my share of hospital visitation over the years. One time, I found myself feeling near to God in the hospital elevator as I was leaving and longed to talk to Him. Suddenly I remembered that most hospitals have a prayer chapel, so I found it and spent time in prayer before moving on to my other activities. I've also used the prayer chapel in airports from time to time. Spaces and places—they keep prayer interesting.

A Personal Style of Prayer

Competition and inferiority can easily slip into the activity of prayer. The Bible warns God followers that "we do not dare to classify or compare ourselves with some who commend themselves. When they measure themselves by themselves and compare themselves with themselves, they are not wise" (2 Corinthians 10:12). Yet we can't help but notice that some people simply find prayer much easier than others. Their passion is high. They're actively engaged. When a prayer meeting is scheduled, they will to be there, on time and ready while others seem to struggle to pray much at all. What's that about?

The reasons for these differences can be practical. Some people are just more verbal and articulate, and it spills over into ease in finding words for prayer. Some have come through dark waters where prayer got them through, and they've developed a "prayer muscle" and an experiential appreciation for prayer. Some carry more burdens and the need for prayer is high. Whatever the differences, be yourself and don't beat up yourself if prayer doesn't come as easily for you as it appears to come for others. Let yourself off the hook to be like someone else who prays and develop your own style and rhythm.

When you notice people who seem to pray easily in public and spend more time in prayer than you, thank God for them. Resist the temptation to see them as specialists even if a title or label comes their way like "intercessor" or "prayer warrior." See them as colleagues, other Christ-followers who pray, like you, and don't be intimidated. God wants to hear *from you* and speak *to you* no matter how many other people are engaged in prayer. No one can do your praying for you.

Motivated to Pray

Over the years, I've been motivated to pray by a variety of things. The logic that God knows about situations, circumstances, and people and I don't is a huge motivator to share my life with Him. The friendship I enjoy with God grows as I spend time with Him. The needs in my life and the lives of those I love drive me to prayer. When I read in Scripture the many stories of men and women who prayed and how it positively affected their lives, I'm motivated to pray. When I realize Jesus is the Son of God and part of the Trinity and still needed to, chose to, and benefited greatly from a lifestyle of consistent prayer while on the earth, I remind myself how much more I need to see prayer as a valuable necessity in my life. Jesus is our great example, including His commitment to prayer.

Let yourself off the hook to be like someone else who prays and develop your own style and rhythm.

I'm also highly motivated to pray when I think of prayer as a beautiful act of submission. When we pray, "Thy will be done," we admit that God is in charge and we are not. This clarifies our priorities. He is sovereign; we are submitted. Throughout the Bible we see a God who guides His children to pray.

Why? Because we *need* to pray. We need His guidance and power and transformation in our lives. Without His help we will mess up and miss out on His best for us. He has consistently taught His children that when we are stymied and struggling He will provide solutions and strategies for us.

Leveling the Praying Field

In sports, there's just too many of us who watch, but never get out on the field. With prayer, don't choose to just sit in the stands. Everyone can pray.

Through prayer we are restored, and we grow in grace and knowledge (2 Peter 3:18). We learn to trust God for the answers we don't see. We learn to know His thoughts, and we share our thoughts with Him. For the believer, prayer is not optional. After more than three decades as a pastor, I truly know prayer to be the best work of anything we can give our time and attention to.

Questions for Reflection

1 What are two or three things that motivate you to pray?

2 What comparisons about prayer do you make with others that you want to stop making?

3 What places of prayer work well for you?

4 Since prayer is talking with God and hearing from Him, what do you know about God that can give you more confidence to pray?

5 Can we sustain a relationship without communication? How does this apply to our relationship with our Heavenly Father?

6 Why is prayer not optional for believers?

2

The Reason
People Don't Pray

*"In prayer have no other motive than to
know your Father in heaven."*

—Oswald Chambers

While this book was percolating in my heart and mind, which has been over the course of several years, I struck up an intriguing conversation with the woman sitting next to me on an airplane. Turns out she is a quite famous author of dark mystery novels, and I was eager to gather some writing tips from her. "What do you keep in mind that helps you most as a writer?" I asked with a desire to learn for my own interest.

"My husband understands and makes space for me to arise in the morning and head straight for my writing desk before my mind gets distracted and cluttered. If I try to write later in the day, nothing happens." Then she asked me, "If you were to write a book what would be the topic?"

Without hesitation, I shared with her that I was in fact writing a book on prayer and welcomed her honesty about her own perspective on the subject. "The reason people don't pray is because it doesn't work," she said. "Oh, it might bring peace to the person praying because they've given voice to their concerns and meditation never hurts. But it's not how I find peace."

Her words lingered in my mind long after we parted ways. Though she made it clear she wasn't a follower of Christ, the backdrop of that conversation is one shared by many people who are. Though they don't say aloud what I heard from the author on the plane, they too believe prayer doesn't work because they haven't seen the results they planned for.

Maybe people who draw the conclusion that prayer doesn't work do so simply because events don't turn out the way they suggested to God would be the best outcome for that situation. You know how it goes. A child prays for a parent to quit drinking, but nothing changes. You want that perfect job, prayed and asked others to pray, only to have it go to someone else. You pray for physical healing repeatedly, but the illness lingers. If we approach prayer like a wish list for Santa Claus, we might be disappointed.

> Prayer is the communication platform we use to keep in touch with the heart of our Lord and Friend, Christ Jesus.

The Bible says, "And we are confident that he hears us whenever we ask for anything that pleases him" (1 John 5:14, NLT). So maybe a "wish list" style of praying has it backwards. Consider that prayer is the communication platform we use to keep in touch with the heart of our Lord and Friend, Christ Jesus. Out of that time spent talking and listening (prayer), we become familiar with what pleases Him. As we tune in to what pleases Him, we find ourselves asking for what we carry in our heart that is also in His heart and in alignment with His will.

God's Timing Is Different from Ours

Sometimes we conclude prayer doesn't work simply because our timetable is different from God's. Just as snow has been released from heaven long before the white flakes touch our nose then our toes, God is always at work on our behalf and His timing is not the same as ours. In fact, He lives outside of time. I'm amazed and encouraged by the people listed in the Faith Hall of Fame in Hebrews 11. Each of them walked in faith yet didn't see the fullness of what God was doing in the moment of obedience. Rather, the fruit of their faithfulness came much later, for some after their life on earth. Notice the delay, and notice God's timetable:

> Sometimes we conclude prayer doesn't work simply because our timetable is different from God's.

- "By faith Noah, when warned about things not yet seen, in holy fear built an ark to save his family" (verse 7).
- "By faith Abraham, when called to go to a place he would later receive as his inheritance, obeyed and went, even though he did not know where he was going" (verse 8).
- "By faith even Sarah, who was past childbearing age, was enabled to bear children because she considered him faithful who had made the promise" (verse 11).
- "By faith the people passed through the Red Sea as on dry land; but when the Egyptians tried to do so, they were drowned" (verse 29).
- "By faith the walls of Jericho fell, after the army had marched around them for seven days" (verse 30).

Does prayer work? That's a difficult question to process in the contemporary spiritual arena filled with type-A personalities, and books and seminars focused on topics such as time management, best practices, and corporate success. What if we turned the whole topic on its head and prayed out of obedience to the Bible, following the strong model demonstrated by Jesus and other men and women of faith in the Bible? What if we prayed to foster a relationship with our Heavenly Father?

God Always Responds to Prayer

One day I was wrestling in my mind and discussing with God whether the priority we were putting on prayer in our church was necessary. It seemed to me the visible fruit wasn't lining up. I would say to our people, "Prayer is the best work," yet I wanted to be able to point to evidence of that. God answered me in that mental wrestling with a clear statement that has helped me ever since: "I could do incredible things in response to your prayers if you would simply give up the need to see the results." That was a turning point for me. I understood my part was to talk to God and hear from Him (pray), and He would be faithful to respond whether I saw His response or whether it ever happened in my lifetime.

If God has given each of us the assignment to pray and share our petitions with Him, can't we trust Him to do His part? It's so easy to be an armchair quarterback and say what we would do if we were on the field. In the spiritual arena, we're tempted to suggest to God how it would be best for Him to answer our prayers. But what if we joined the men and women from the Faith Hall of Fame and trusted God and

> If God has given each of us the assignment to pray and share our petitions with Him, can't we trust Him to do His part?

His great love for us as His children even when the results of our prayers are different from what we expected?

The very question "Does prayer work?" puts a misplaced emphasis on prayer as a communication avenue and on the word *work*, as if it were a formula. Instead, it helps me to say, "My God is who He says He is, and I have the privilege to talk to Him and hear from Him."

I have a life coach in another state with whom I meet by FaceTime or Zoom. When I recently referred my coach to a friend, I talked about the coach's qualities and why I like her as a coach. After my conversations with the life coach, I think about the goals we've set, the substance of those conversations, and the admirable person she is. I've said to myself and others comments about this person like "What an effective coach," or I've made observations about our discussions like "That was a helpful session." I've never once said, "Skype works" or "FaceTime works" when giving a glowing report about this coaching relationship.

Yet when we talk about God, we can get overly focused on the communication tool instead of the Person to whom we speak and the conversations we enjoy. When we say things like "I felt the prayers," maybe what we really mean is we felt God's help and closeness in response to your prayers for us. Or when we say, "Prayer works," maybe what we mean is that God helps us when we talk to Him. When a person says, "Prayer doesn't work," maybe what they mean is God responded differently than they expected or hoped.

Pray with Confidence

God is who He says He is, and we get to talk to Him and hear from Him. He is:

- The Way, the Truth, and the Life (John 14:6)
- Love (1 John 4:8, 16)
- The First and the Last, the Beginning and the End (Revelation 22:13)
- The hope of eternal life who does not lie (Titus 1:2)
- The Rock whose works are perfect (Deuteronomy 32:4)
- Creator of all things (Colossians 1:16)
- God of the impossible (Luke 18:27)
- Ever-present, merciful God (Deuteronomy 4:31)
- The great equalizer (Galatians 3:28)
- Strong to help us (Isaiah 41:10)

James Hudson Taylor said, "When we work, we work. When we pray, God works." God works even if we can't see the change or it's not in our timing. His mercy and grace give us what He desires for our lives. So, do we just keep on praying even when it appears not to make any difference? Absolutely! Here's what we know for sure. There's no doubt that every Christian is supposed to pray.

> God works even if we can't see the change or it's not in our timing.

No argument could ever be made using the Bible that prayer is optional or a special assignment for a few. Prayer is to every Christian what breathing is to a body.

But don't I have a right to see the answers to my prayers? Well, not really. Sometimes it happens that we see answers and it gives us encouragement and something to celebrate. But imagine how strong your prayer life would become if you gave up the right or the need to see the results. Absolutely, we can trust God to do what is His will to do when we pray. But our human limitations of time and location and perspective keep us from seeing what God is doing in response to our prayers. Sure, God is responding. But we don't always see what He sees.

I totally get it that a testimony of answered prayer can really boost one's faith and motivate us toward prayer. I think a full 360° view of prayer includes praying to give—not always to get—and leaving the results to God.

Prayer works if we're praying according to God's will and leaving the results up to Him. We aren't in charge, He is—and we can trust Him. It takes a mature person to give your best energy to an investment like prayer that is private before the Lord, knowing the results may or may not be measurable within your view and within your lifetime.

"These were all commended for their faith, yet none of them received what had been promised, since God had planned something better for us so that only together with us would they be made perfect" (Hebrews 11:39–40). God can be trusted to have "something better" for us if we'll patiently trust Him beyond what we can see immediately.

On the playing field, what if we played like we were winning even if the scoreboard were covered? On the praying field, what if we prayed with confidence that God is responding even when we can't see the results? What if we gave up the need to be the arbiters of God's will because we understand that His plans are far above anything our most astute minds could dream up?

"For my thoughts are not your thoughts, neither are your ways my ways," declares the LORD. "As the heavens are higher than the earth, so are my ways higher than your ways and my thoughts than your thoughts" (Isaiah 55:8–9).

When there's a good team leader, each person on the team only needs to carry out the assignment given to them and the group wins.

General Motors makes cars on an assembly line. There may be an employee who puts four bolts on the floorboards of cars all day long but never gets to see the finished shiny car on the showroom floor. If he faithfully completes his assignment, he knows he helped to build that final product. In a similar way, we're on God's team and our assignment is to pray for His purposes to be fulfilled. We need to pray faithfully, knowing we have a Creator God who is doing His part to answer our prayers.

Questions for Reflection

1 When you remind yourself who God is and reflect on His attributes, how does that impact your prayers?

2 Share an experience where God responded to your prayer in an obvious way. What effect did this have on you?

3 What is satisfying to you about prayer other than receiving an obvious, immediate answer to your prayer?

4 How would you pray if your goal was to see God's will accomplished?

5 Do you find it difficult to submit to God's wisdom for the answers to your prayers? Why or why not?

3

Location, Location, Location

"Our prayers release God's will into our world."

—Jeff Leake

If you're opening a new restaurant, buying a house, or planting a church, one of the three most important factors to consider is location, location, location. So, what does that have to do with prayer? The place we pray is important on many levels. When developing a habit of prayer, it can be helpful to find a certain quiet spot that becomes your place of prayer. That doesn't mean you're limited to that place. On the contrary, because we can touch the heart of God anywhere at any time, we aren't restricted to praying in a certain location. Beyond that, our prayers can be effective in a special way when we pray in close proximity to the prayer topic.

This happened one Wednesday night

when I was a youth pastor. The service was based on Acts 19:18–19: "Many who became believers confessed their sinful practices. A number of them who had been practicing sorcery brought their incantation books and burned them at a public bonfire" (NLT).

At the time, several students in our youth group had brought items to the youth leaders that they felt God wanted them to remove from their lives. So, we invited the whole youth group to take time to consider things in their lives that might be offensive to the Lord or might hold them back in their walk with God. We invited them to bring those items on a given Wednesday night for an outdoor service on location and throw them in the "public bonfire" with a prayer of repentance to follow.

Students brought weed and other drugs, pornography and posters, memorabilia from relationships they needed to leave in the past, cigarettes, and whatever needed to go. Praying on location beside a bonfire and physically participating in those outward steps with the support of others around them had a huge impact on those students. That and many similar experiences have convinced me that prayers on location can make a significant difference.

Consider the life of Christ for examples of prayer on location. Yes, He prayed in the temple, but He didn't limit prayer to that location. He prayed in a boat on a raging sea, in a garden, among the tombstones, in the wilderness, and on a cross, just to name a few. Let's look at how Jesus prayed in some rather unusual places:

- When Jesus and His disciples were out on the Sea of Galilee and a raging storm suddenly threatened to capsize their boat, Jesus prayed for the sea to be calm (Matthew 8:23–27).

- When Jesus was walking in the region of the Gadarenes and two demon-possessed men approached Him from the tombs, He prayed for the demons to come out of them (Matthew 8:28–34).
- After John baptized Jesus in the Jordan River, Jesus went into the wilderness to fast and pray for forty days in preparation for His ministry (Matthew 4:1–11).
- When Jesus was dying on the cross for our sins, He prayed for His Heavenly Father to forgive those who were killing Him (Luke 23:34).

We aren't limited to a church setting when we pray but are free to pray where our prayers can do the most good and where we can most effectively connect our hearts with the need.

Mark Batterson, lead pastor of the National Community Church in Washington, DC, shares in his book *The Circle Maker* how he walked over four miles through the streets of our nation's capital and prayed for God to guide him in planting a church there. God answered his prayers in surprising ways:

> Without even knowing it, I walked right by a piece of property at 8th Street and Virginia Avenue SE that we would purchase thirteen years later as a result of a $3 million gift that wasn't even a prayer yet. Without even knowing it, I walked right under a theater marquee on Barracks Row, the main street of Capitol Hill, that we would renovate and reopen as our seventh location fifteen years later.[1]

Was it important that he pray on location? Absolutely! Like the Israelites who marched around Jericho and prayed for the walls to fall, Mark walked

> **We aren't limited to a church setting when we pray but are free to pray where our prayers can do the most good and where we can most effectively connect our hearts with the need.**

around Washington, DC, and prayed for God to help him plant a church. God answered his prayers with not one church, but seven! Location matters.

When we heard the Republican National Convention was coming to Cleveland in 2016, our church began to consider how God might want us to respond. Our building was on the outskirts of Cleveland proper, in a bedroom community just minutes from the Quicken Loans Arena where the convention would be held.

What opportunity for ministry would that bring our way? Any large event, whether a Super Bowl or convention, causes an increase in human trafficking, thus an opportunity for ministry. We teamed up with a nearby ministry that specializes in freeing those trapped in human trafficking, Rahab Ministries, and took their lead on how to proceed. They provided training and guidance to let our church be the hub of hosting groups that traveled from other parts of the United States to be a part of this outreach. Teams went out to do a prayer walk and interact with women at the fourteen hotels in the area.

What were the results? Well, part of maturing in prayer is to be obedient and leave the results to God, but when He pulled back the curtain and gave us a glimpse of answers to our prayers we were thrilled. We heard from law enforcement of riots that didn't happen, close calls that were averted, and an unusual sense of peace and calm in the area instead of the riots that had been forecast. Other results that can't be shared publicly let us know God was actively at work in response to prayers. This experience reminded us that God works where we can't see results and His assignment for us to pray-walk that location was right on track.

God Is Everywhere

Praying on location helps us see what's going on in that place and enables us to carry the Spirit of God into that space. Praying on location engages the unseen Spirit of God with the unseen spiritual activity in that space and pushes back the spiritual darkness. "For our struggle is not against flesh and blood, but against the rulers, against the authorities, against the powers of this dark world and against the spiritual forces of evil in the heavenly realms" (Ephesians 6:12). There's a battle to be won in the unseen environment and praying on location is a great way to fight the fight.

God is everywhere. He can hear our prayers from the side of our bed or the altar of a sanctuary, but as I often shared with our congregation when we prayed for missionaries in foreign lands, "We can travel anywhere on our knees." Let me encourage you not to miss out on the benefits of praying on location when the opportunity presents itself and you feel God prompting you to do so.

Coaching for Pastors

During my time as associate pastor at Bethel Christian Church in Parma, Ohio, I was preparing to offer a Wednesday night elective on the topic of my choice. The topic would be prayer, and I wanted it to draw out people for the best thirteen-week series they would ever experience! Prayer should be the most exciting thing that happens in a church, yet it can be difficult to inspire enthusiasm in others, so I implemented an idea I hoped would spark a new and renewed interest in prayer.

I reserved the church minibus and urged the attendees to bring their coats and boots because we would be going "on location" (winter in Cleveland). We were gone and back within ninety minutes since family members were in youth group, the nursery, and other electives. We opened the session in the church with a few Scriptures, comments, and directions, then got on the bus and went on location to pray.

Our locations included the local community college, hospital, police station, fire department, and city hall. Our county had a large Muslim mosque, so we prayed in its parking lot. We prayed at the middle school, two high school campuses, and prayed through some neighborhoods and business areas. What better way to see your own community, exegete the culture, and pray for them than going together on location?

Praying on Location with People

When we're willing to pray on location, we pray *now* and *with* a person rather than *later* and *for* a person. A staff member, Cathy, and I were leaving Aladdin's Café after lunch when we bumped into one of her friends, so she introduced the two of us. The friend's response to "How are you?" moved quickly to the burden that was obviously on the tip of her tongue as she shared a desperate situation about her mom's health. Cathy listened with compassion and quickly responded, "Oh, I'm so sorry to hear that. I'll pray for you." Then with just a few seconds of a pause, she added, "In fact, would you mind if we prayed with you right here?"

"Oh, that would be wonderful!" her friend responded. Right there on the sidewalk of the plaza the three of us joined in prayer, followed by a tearful hug of gratitude from the friend. That time of prayer was completely natural, spontaneous, and sincere. When people are in desperate situations, they welcome prayer and are comforted to hear you talk to God on their behalf.

A few weeks later another friend and I were enjoying lunch in the outdoor patio of a restaurant. We bumped into some Christian friends with a difficult situation in their lives, and they asked if we would pray with them, which we gladly did.

When we had finished praying, a man sitting at a table nearby motioned for us to come over to his table. "I saw you are people of prayer, and I wondered if you would pray for me." It was about a job situation, and his eyes welled with tears as he shared the need with us. People are desperate for a connection with God, and they can quickly set aside any sense of self-consciousness when there's an opportunity for prayer.

Another time my sister and I were having dinner in downtown Cleveland when I noticed a couple I casually knew at a table across the restaurant. I had read on Facebook that they were in Cleveland because he was facing surgery at the clinic. We were in a bit of a hurry, but as we passed their table and chatted briefly, I sensed God prompt me to offer for my sister and me to have prayer with them for what they were facing. They gladly accepted, and we prayed together at their table.

As we walked away, I was struck with the serendipity of that encounter. It was like a light went on that God is often an unseen guest who is longing to be included in our conversations. Praying with people on location can easily become part of the flow of our day. God is continuously placing people in our paths who are hungry for an encounter with God and need a touch from Him. I would like to think that instead of seeing such events as rare occasions, we assume that our encounters are designed by God and should include Him unless He specifically prompts us otherwise.

Leveling the Praying Field

To stop and pray on location with whomever is in the circle is a great exercise in leveling the praying field because everyone can participate. It's not something that is relegated to a church building and carried out only by members of the clergy, but is an act of love and concern that every follower of Christ can do.

Questions for Reflection

1 Do you think a person can pray anywhere and God will hear? Explain why or why not.

2 How can praying on location bring emphasis and urgency to the prayer?

3 When we pray for people on location, how can the Holy Spirit help us to pray wisely?

4 Can you think of times when the apostles prayed on location? Make a list of these events, then let it guide and encourage you.

5 Do you think that praying on location can be a step of faith? Explain how.

4

What Matters Most Is Who Is on the Other End of the "Line"

"We must not decide how to pray based on what types of prayer are the most effective for producing the experience and feelings we want. We pray in response to God Himself."

—Timothy Keller

When circumstances turn out the way a person asked in prayer, they'll often say, "Prayer works." Think of prayer as the telephone, a communication device. What really matters is who is on the other end of the line. Think about this: We're praying to the Creator of the universe. Our God, who is the Way, the Truth, and the Life (John 14:6), is the One to whom we pray, who is ever present, all-powerful, all-knowing, always existing, not bound by time. "God's Son shines out with God's glory, and all that God's Son is and does marks him as God" (Hebrews 1:3, TLB). Our God is the One who sticks closer than a brother (Proverbs 18:24) and is the perfect Father and friend. If we weren't communicating with Him, there would be no point to pray. He is the reason we pray.

> **The focal point is that we pray to Creator God in the name of Jesus.**

The truth of this dawned on me one day as I was visiting with some of my neighbors. The apartment complex where I lived in Cleveland, Ohio, allowed a group of residents to use the clubhouse for an English-as-a-Second-Language class. Linda was the teacher, and I was one of a few volunteers. The daytime class, made up of women whose husbands were at work, were from Turkey, India, and China, and each was either Hindu or Muslim. They had studied English in the classroom, but wanted to learn conversational English, accents, and idioms. They also wanted help with cultural issues like how to get a library card, visit the doctor, and use 911.

Over the course of time we developed close friendships. We went on field trips together, learned and sang Christmas carols, and shared meals in one another's homes. If I said, "I'll pray for you about that," they would respond, "I'll pray, too." Prayer was the common activity, but for me the light went on when I realized that what mattered most was the one to whom each person prayed.

One day during Ramadan (the month of fasting in Islam), our Muslim friends invited several of us to their home for the meal that breaks the daily fast at sunset. We enjoyed talking about our different faiths and sharing mutual traditions.

As we ate a delicious meal, we discussed the purpose of their fast. When the time came for their evening prayer, our hostess rolled her prayer mat on the floor in a prescribed direction and knelt with her face to the floor to pray toward Mecca, a holy city for Muslims. I admired her boldness and commitment. I loved the opportunity it gave all of us to share, including the Christians at the table who talked about the One to whom we pray: Jesus Christ as Son of God, Forgiver of sins, Friend, and Comforter.

This experience helped me understand that prayer is the communication tool and the focal point is that we pray to Creator God in the name of Jesus. This thought has challenged my thinking to move beyond glibly saying, "Prayer works," to think about the person of Jesus Christ who acts in response to our talking to Him and hearing from Him. Among friends who aren't Christ-followers, it became more evident to me that to say, "Prayer works" or "I've been praying for you," was unclear and stopped short of giving credit to Jesus Christ. Rather than referring to prayer, why not take it a step further and talk about the activity of the God to whom we pray? So, I began saying things like, "Jesus Christ is helping Dave recover from his injuries in response to prayer." "I'm so thankful to the Lord Jesus for saving my friends' marriage." "When I pray, Jesus helps me have greater compassion for my coworker."

> We do not pray to an unknown god, but to the God who has revealed Himself through His Son Jesus, His Holy Spirit, and His Word.

Keep the Focus on the Triune God

We pray to a living, personal triune God who wants to be our friend. We do not pray to an unknown god, but to the God who has revealed Himself through His Son Jesus, His Holy Spirit, and His Word. We pray to the one true God who has demonstrated His love and concern throughout history. We have no reason to doubt that He hears

our prayers and speaks to us, and we must understand this ourselves as we pray and make it clear to
others who hear us pray.

Let's consider some basic truths about the One
to whom we pray, the God of the Bible:

- God is by nature infinite, without limit or limitation. He is greater than the universe, for He created it (1 Kings 8:27).
- God is at the same time both transcendent (above, beyond, and greater than the universe He has created) and immanent (present and active in our own lives) (Psalm 135:5–6; 46:1).
- God's nature doesn't change, and never will (see Malachi 3:6).
- God is omnipotent, all-powerful, and is sovereign over the universe (Isaiah 40:15).
- God is omnipresent, everywhere present at once. He isn't limited by space (Psalm 139:7–10).
- God is omniscient, having infinite, universal,

complete knowledge and insight. All reality is known to Him. All events, past, present, and future, are available to Him as present knowledge (Romans 8:27–28; 1 Corinthians 3:20).

- God is truly a good God. Evil is an enemy of both creation and God. The Bible is filled with descriptions of God's goodness, people ascribing to Him such characteristics as love (1 John 4:8), loving-kindness and faithfulness (Psalm 89:49), grace (Acts 20:24), and mercy (Ephesians 2:4).
- God is holy (Isaiah 6:1–5). [2]

When we understand the nature of God, we pray with confidence and with humility. We know He is powerful to answer our prayers. We also know He is Lord of the universe, and we stand in awe that He would hear our prayers.

Think Differently about Prayer

It may seem paradoxical, but the more I learned from my Hindu friends how they pray to a variety of hundreds of gods and each family selects a few favorites, the more I realized what an honor and holy privilege it is to have a real and personal relationship with the one, true God.

Another religious discipline we have in common is fasting, which my Hindu neighbor did faithfully every Tuesday. We invited one another to our homes and talked about our faiths and shared together. My Hindu friend used her kitchen pantry as a prayer altar with statues of gods and candles. When it was time for a special festival, she invited me to come see it. Other times the family cleared out the living room and created a makeshift altar with candles, plates for food offered to the god, and a statue of the god that was the focus of that festival. Their guests passed through the living room, expressed their honor to the god, and enjoyed food together. Eventually, the leader called the people together, read from a book, burned incense, and said a prayer.

Hanging out with people who prayed and fasted, yet were not Christians, caused me to think differently about prayer and to communicate differently about

Jesus. The focus of prayer and fasting shifted beyond the action to the One to whom I pray: Creator God, in the name of His Son Jesus Christ with whom I have a personal relationship that assures me of my eternal destiny and brings me abundant life while living for Him on this earth.

As these Hindu friends visited the church I pastored, I became more mindful of my choice of words. Similarly, guests who were active in Alcoholics Anonymous came from a culture where they were encouraged to pray to a "higher power" of their choice. I could no longer assume that just because we were praying, we were all aiming in the same direction.

> **Hanging out with people who prayed and fasted, yet were not Christians, caused me to think differently about prayer and to communicate differently about Jesus.**

When I hosted friends for a meal in my house, I politely informed them that it was my custom to pray before a meal. They were always glad for us to pray together. I would also let them know I prayed to only one God and my God is Jesus Christ. Sometimes I would break that down a little more in conversations about the one God expressed in three Persons: Father, Son, and Holy Spirit.

We can't assume others know who we talk to when we pray, so we must be clear about this. My neighbor was concerned about her baby not taking nourishment and failing to thrive. I listened with compassion and asked about medical appointments, etc. Then I asked if it would be okay if

> **For the follower of Christ, prayer is a communication tool by which we talk to God and hear from God, the God of the Bible, in the name of Jesus.**

I prayed for her son:

Friend: Sure, that would be great. Thank you.

Me: To be clear, I pray to the God of the Bible, God the Father, in the name of Jesus Christ. Is that okay with you?

Friend: Sure, that's fine.

For some religions, prayer is a series of words repeated to a variety of gods with the belief that this develops favor and prevents punishment or anger from the gods. For the follower of Christ, prayer is a communication tool by which we talk to God and hear from God, the God of the Bible, in the name of Jesus. We pray to develop and foster a personal relationship with our Heavenly Father, receive forgiveness of sin, learn His heart and will for our lives, express our concerns, hear His love for us, and share our love with Him, and so much more. This living, active God is the focus of prayer, which is the communication tool.

Leveling the Praying Field

Keep in mind, prayer isn't an activity that earns us favor with God, but is the communication tool to develop a relationship with Him in the name of our wonderful Savior! As you interact with others in prayer, don't assume everyone listening is on the same page with you.

Questions for Reflection

1 Have you interacted with someone who serves a god different from the God you serve? How does prayer enter the picture for them?

2 Can a person do the activity of prayer without relationally connecting with the god to whom they pray?

3 How might you consider saying it differently to more clearly give glory to God in place of phrases such as "Prayer works" or "I felt the prayers"?

4 How does it increase your desire to pray when you know you pray to the powerful God who created the universe?

5 How can gaining more knowledge of God from His Word encourage us to pray more often and to believe for answers to our prayers?

5

Practical Tools for Prayer

"Jesus immersed His words and work in prayer. Powerful things happen when we do the same."

—Max Lucado

It is my personal belief that every minister or person in the people-helping business should have a counselor on speed dial to touch base with as needed. In my life, a Christian counselor named Pam was one of the dear people who helped me grow in my prayer life. In our discussions, she frequently asked me, "What is God saying to you about that?" Truth be told, I wasn't sure I was hearing from God at all. So, I asked her to show me what "hearing from God" might look like.

"Well, here's what it looks like for me," she said. "I have a prayer chair I visit every morning where I bring a cup of coffee, my Bible, and my prayer journal."

I was puzzled. "Your prayer journal? Tell me about that. "

Pam explained. "It's just an ordinary lined, blank journal I bought at a stationery store. I write in blue ink the words I want to say to the Lord in prayer. There's something helpful about taking the time to write it out longhand. Then I wait in God's presence for what I sense He is saying in response to what I've written. When I get a sense of His response, I write it in red. Back and forth we have a discussion, in blue ink and red ink."

> "Over the course of time I've learned to hear His voice, to recognize the ideas He drops in my heart while I wait on Him."

This raised an obvious question for me. "How do you know those impressions in your mind are from God and not just something your mind has made up?"

Without hesitation, Pam replied, "God's response always lines up with the Word of God and the nature of God. Over the course of time I've learned to hear His voice, to recognize the ideas He drops in my heart while I wait on Him. The Enemy wouldn't be telling me the type of things I write."

Red-Pen Journaling

Red-pen journaling became a habit I picked up from Pam that I'm still practicing more than twenty years later. What a great record to refer back to for encouragement! When I tend to wander off-point or forget why I'm doing what I'm doing in my daily life, I find it encouraging to go back to my journal and read what God was telling me and then remind myself of the conversation the two of us had about specific issues.

Words of Others

Another way God speaks to me is through the words of another person or a message I hear or something I read in the Bible. When God impresses something specific on my heart, I write it in my prayer journal. In our high-tech world of information overload, God's voice is the only one that matters, and we need to develop the ability to hear Him clearly and often.

> In our high-tech world of information overload, God's voice is the only one that matters, and we need to develop the ability to hear Him clearly and often.

Whatever you've found to be helpful in hearing God's voice, be willing to allow others to peek over your shoulder and learn from you. Take time to show them what it looks like. Likewise, if you know someone who seems to hear clearly from the Lord, don't hesitate to ask them how they hear from Him and how they foster that two-way conversation daily.

When it comes to resourcing, have you set aside funds to purchase tools such as books, videos, seminars etc., to strengthen your prayer life or to fund retreats and prayer activities? When pastors and church boards include prayer in the church budget, this provides resources, promotions, guest speakers, etc., for prayer events in the church. There are so many creative ways to enhance the prayer experiences for your church, but it takes funding, scheduling, and planning ahead.

One year I took a group from the church I was pastoring on a field trip to the Tuesday evening prayer meeting at Brooklyn Tabernacle in New York City. Pastor Jim Cymbala is a favorite author and seems to be leading the way in prayer as a pastor. I can't tell you how amazing it was for our group to see a few thousand people come out on Tuesday night, many riding public transit, to pray together. This experience raised the level of prayer intensity in our church and especially inspired me. Was it worth the time it took to plan and prepare and the resources spent to carry it out? Absolutely!

Another time I took a field trip to the International House of Prayer in Kansas City, Missouri, and discovered a fantastic learning experience for me as a pastor. These prayer events won't happen without intentional planning and budgeting.

Similarly, it's telling of a church or ministry to consider where prayer lines up in their calendar of events and on their website. If you're the leader of a church, ask yourself how easy it is for a person who attends your church to find opportunities to pray, to be prayed for, and to learn about prayer. Are there regular times on the calendar when prayer happens intentionally? Are there special times of prayer emphasis throughout the year that members can look forward to and plan for? Reflect honestly on how much time and effort and funds your church has set aside for prayer endeavors.

The rhythm of prayer I developed for the church I pastored went something like this:

- Block off a Week of Prayer the first full week of the new year with nightly 7 p.m. prayer services.

- Block off forty days of Seek God for the City from Ash Wednesday through Palm Sunday.

- Block off a Week of Prayer in the fall for a special purpose.

- Book prayer/worship Friday night services periodically.

- Maintain preservice prayer forty-five minutes before each Sunday morning service. People knew they could come early before the service to receive prayer or to join a group of others to pray for the church, the city, and that morning's service. Any of our supported missionaries knew they could e-mail special or urgent prayer requests and we would pray for them during this time.

Prioritize Prayer Time

As I said in chapter 1, I find two things telling of a person's values: their calendar and their financial record (checkbook/budget). If you look back over the last seven days of your calendar or look forward to the next seven days, are there intentional appointments of prayer?

Personal Prayer Retreat

On a personal level, I booked personal overnight prayer retreats quarterly at an isolated spot (for example, a cabin at our campground or in a state park, a friend's condo near the beach, or a friend's home an hour away from mine). These multiday retreats were vital times of spiritual renewal for me. At times I collected prayer requests from the congregation to take with me. Other times I prayed through the church directory for people's needs.

Work Six Days, Rest One

In addition to daily times of prayer, the biblical prescription of work six days and rest one day is a good rhythm for rest, prayer, and spiritual refreshment. As a pastor, Fridays seemed to work best for that day of rest. And if for some reason an event got scheduled on a Friday, I would immediately look for a nearby day as an alternative. The example and instruction of our Lord to work six days and rest one day is not just a command—it's a gift!

Resources

There are many great prayer resources available today and these are more easily accessible than ever before through the Internet. One great source of prayer guides is www.waymakers.org. This organization provides a wide variety of prayer guides on various topics that can be a tremendous help to you as an individual or to an entire church. One prayer guide, *Seek God for the City*, covers a forty-day focus from Ash Wednesday through Palm Sunday with a weekly theme. Each day covers a Scripture to pray and a group of people to pray for (such as first responders, single moms, educators, etc.). It organizes prayer for other countries by region, and then follows with about six countries a day in alphabetical order. We found this such a helpful tool for our church that we began buying extra copies and gifting them to city council members and educators. We even placed them in the public library for people to take for free. One year I spoke for the Kiwanis Club and incorporated the prayer guide into my talk. I took enough copies to give one to each person and received an overwhelming response of gratitude for this resource.

> In addition to daily times of prayer, the biblical prescription of work six days and rest one day is a good rhythm for rest, prayer, and spiritual refreshment.

Another great resource for books and a wide variety of material on prayer is My Healthy Church with the Assemblies of God (MyHealthyChurch. com). The magazine *PRAY!* is one I've subscribed to and used for many years. The plus side of this age of technology is that we're gifted with tools to enhance our prayer times. At the touch of my cell phone, here are some favorite prayer apps I've loaded to enjoy:

- Seek God for the City from waymakers.org
- Pray the Word
- IHOPKC (International House of Prayer in Kansas City)
- Abide

Authors who have published exceptional work on prayer include Dick Eastman, Jim Cymbala, Mike Bickle, E. M. Bounds, Richard Foster, A. W. Tozer, R. A. Torrey, Watchman Nee, Leonard Ravenhill, and Corrie ten Boom.

The main character in the movie *War Room* is a great example of a believer who understood her role as a Christian and the power we all have when we bear down in focused, consistent, desperate prayer. She also understood the value of leveling the praying field for the young wife who also needed to war in prayer for her own marriage. She didn't set herself up saying, "Let me go to the war room in prayer for you" but rather "Come and see. I'll equip you and join you in your war."

Leveling the Praying Field

When our military goes to battle, it's not based on a casual, hit-or-miss approach, but on a deliberate strategy that's discussed and monitored in the war room. Similarly, our spiritual engagement with God through personal prayer requires an equal level of intentionality and monitoring. I hope these resources and ideas will help you put a prayer plan in place that's unique for you and your church. Let it be an action plan with specific goals, appointments, and a strategy that will pull you into a deeper place of prayer than you've ever known.

Questions for Reflection

1 What method or strategy has helped you have a quality time of prayer almost daily?

2 What method or strategy described in this chapter might be one you would like to try?

3 What individuals have helped you to mature in prayer?

4 Who are a few people in your world who might be a good prayer mentor or partner for you going forward?

6

Connect Directly with God's Spirit in Prayer

"When we pray in the Spirit with the Fire of God directing us, we pray in harmony with the perfect will of God . . . and incredible things happen."

—Scott Wilson and John Bates

My friend Nancy has been a strong influence in helping my prayer life to grow. This started when she provided access to her second home as a place where I could retreat to for times of prayer and rest. When she accompanied me, rather than visiting with me she would intentionally leave me alone to spend time doing what I had come to do, be with Jesus. That made the times we did visit so much richer. We would talk about a study either of us was involved in or watch a video teaching together or get out our iPads and Bibles to explore a Scripture and talk about Jesus. When you find a friendship like that, it's gold!

One conversation that makes me laugh to this day was when Nancy relayed something about her prayer time with God. She was praying about a specific situation, giving detailed information as to how God could resolve the matter. We've all done that, right? She was providing God with details of what she thought would be the best outcome for Him to provide in this prayer need. Yet at some point in her prayer, Nancy heard God say clearly, "Don't tell Me what to do!" We both laughed. That was a turning point in the way she prayed. She turned her focus to "God, be glorified in this situation" rather than "God, here's how I think You should answer this prayer."

The truth is, when we pray, we only have a small part of the story and fuzzy facts based on human understanding. We're limited in the information and can't see into the future to know how this piece of the puzzle might best fit into the whole picture, so to instruct God on the details really seems a bit absurd. Since He has our best interests at heart, knows the future and past, and has all the intelligence about the situation, wouldn't it be great if our spirit could connect directly with His Spirit in prayer and bypass our limited knowledge?

Praying in the Spirit

We can! That's exactly what happens when we pray in tongues. We engage the perfect knowledge of God, connected to our hearts, practically using our voice and bypassing our limited human knowledge. What a power tool! This is one of the wonderful parts I love about being a Pentecostal believer.

In case this is a new concept for you, let me explain further by first sharing some key Bible verses on this subject.

- All of them were filled with the Holy Spirit and began to speak in other tongues as the Spirit enabled them (Acts 2:4).

- When Paul placed his hands on them, the Holy Spirit came on them, and they spoke in tongues and prophesied (Acts 19:6).

- And the Holy Spirit helps us in our weakness. For example, we don't know what God wants us to pray for. But the Holy Spirit prays for us with groanings that cannot be expressed in words. And the Father who knows all hearts knows what the Spirit is saying, for the Spirit pleads for us believers in harmony with God's own will (Romans 8:26–27, NLT).

- If I pray in tongues, my spirit is praying, but I don't understand what I am saying (1 Corinthians 14:14, NLT).

- Pray in the Spirit on all occasions with all kinds of prayers and requests. With this in mind, be alert and always keep

on praying for all the Lord's people (Ephesians 6:18).

- **But you, dear friends, must build each other up in your most holy faith, pray in the power of the Holy Spirit, and await the mercy of our Lord Jesus Christ, who will bring you eternal life. In this way, you will keep yourselves safe in God's love (Jude 20–21, NLT).**

Just to clarify terms as I'm using them, when a person becomes a Christian, the Holy Spirit *enters* their life completely and fully. They have the Holy Spirit in their life at that point of salvation. An additional encounter/interaction with the Holy Spirit that embraces what happened on the Day of Pentecost in the Book of Acts is to seek the *baptism in the Holy Spirit*. There's nothing you can do to earn the Baptism, and it doesn't make a Christian superior to other Christians. It's available for any believer who asks and seeks this experience. We refer to this experience as being filled with the Spirit.

This infilling isn't a requirement for salvation; it's the means of receiving power and guidance from God to live for Him here on earth. The initial sign of being baptized in the Holy Spirit is speaking in tongues, also known as *glossolalia* (Acts 2:4; 1 Corinthians 14:18) or speaking in a language you have never learned. God uses your voice and your tongue to speak a language that comes from heaven. He doesn't overpower you in an experience beyond your control and participation, but works with and through you.

> This infilling isn't a requirement for salvation; it's the means of receiving power and guidance from God to live for Him here on earth.

Sometimes the language is a known earthly language, but more often it's a heavenly language. It's yours to use whenever you want to pray in tongues or in a "prayer language." You can start speaking and stop speaking as you decide. If you're praying with people who don't believe in this experience, you can opt to pray in your known language instead. In fact, praying in the Spirit is both for your individual times of prayer and for prayer with others of similar practice and belief. It's a uniquely personal experience when your spirit prays to God through His Holy Spirit. This isn't to be confused with the experience of giving a message in tongues among a group of believers that needs to be interpreted for the sake of the listeners. (We'll touch on that in chapter 7.)

My Personal Experience

I accepted Christ on a Sunday morning at age fifteen. Several months later I was baptized in the Holy Spirit and spoke in tongues for the first time. I was attending a citywide worship gathering at our local middle school auditorium sponsored by area churches. As the pastor leading the meeting encouraged us to lift our voices to praise, worship, and express our love to the Lord, I did this and my English words suddenly became syllables I had never learned or heard before. I was baptized in the Holy Spirit in that moment without really knowing much about it.

As a young follower of Christ, I was slightly familiar with the experience of speaking in tongues, but I had never spoken in tongues myself. I didn't know enough to be seeking this experience; I was seeking God, and tongues came as a result so I could express myself to Him beyond the limited vocabulary of my own language. When I went home that night, I knelt by my bed and prayed, "Lord, if this is from You, I want it." There beside my bed, I continued to pray to the Lord, but not in known words—I prayed in tongues.

That was my initial experience in using a prayer language. It's a fantastic power tool that I love to make a part of my everyday life. When I pray in tongues, I may have a general topic in the front of my mind, like "wisdom for work" or "healing for Debbie." While that topic might hover there, I will pray in tongues with words that are not mine. I don't know specifically what I'm saying, but I know who I'm seeking. The Spirit of God is praying through me directly, and this helps me pray with wisdom and knowledge beyond myself.

As we seek God, He baptizes us in His Holy Spirit, and we speak in tongues, not as a onetime event but as a tool to help us any time we pray. If this baptism doesn't come the first time you seek it from God, you've still been victorious because you've spent time seeking God. Don't back away or give up. Keep asking for the Baptism and, more importantly, keep seeking the Baptizer, God. After that first encounter with the Spirit of God, we have the choice to speak in tongues (and stop) whenever and wherever we want.

Emotions and Speaking in Tongues

People often ask about the feelings or emotions that come with speaking in tongues. Someone once shared a great illustration about a three-car train to explain this to me. The engine of the train is fact, the second car is faith, and the caboose is feeling. Some people experience a lot of emotion when they seek God and are baptized in His Holy Spirit. Some feel nothing, but their experience is just as real. I've never been one to be led by feelings. What drives my experience are the facts of what the Bible tells us followed by my faith in God that He is true to His Word and His Spirit is real. The feelings come along, or not, as an optional third part, or caboose, of the train. We can't lead with feelings, ignore the facts, and have no faith any more than a train can drive with the caboose and forget about the engine and second car.

Some people feel they can't pray in tongues unless they're feeling the strong emotions that had previously been a part of this Holy Spirit baptism experience for them. Do we need to feel a certain way to pray in the Spirit? Do we need to have strong emotions move us to pray in this way? No. I would suggest we set aside whether the feelings are there and simply pray in tongues. Why? Because this powerful tool from God allows us to communicate with Him beyond our learned language and beyond our human knowledge of the situations for which we are praying.

While talking about emotions, it's important to know that praying in tongues is cathartic and good for the person praying, not only spiritually but emotionally and mentally. Whether you feel depressed, angry, confused, or anxious, spend some time praying in tongues and as you communicate with God who is in the heavenlies, He will bring peace and rest to your soul. Shane, a friend of mine, shared that he processes his anger by getting in his pickup truck, driving to the end of the country road, cranking up his favorite music, and praying in tongues until he feels freedom from his anger.

> This powerful tool from God allows us to communicate with Him beyond our learned language and beyond our human knowledge of the situations for which we are praying.

Dr. Richard Dobbins, founder of the counseling center Emerge Ministries in Akron, Ohio, gave a teaching entitled, "The Mental Health Benefits of Praying in Tongues." A segment of ABC's *Nightline* reported on the science of speaking in tongues:

At the University of Pennsylvania, Dr. Andrew Newberg is looking for an explanation of what many say is unexplainable. It's not normal language that would typically activate the frontal lobe. Newberg is exploring the relationship between faith and science, studying what happens to the brain during the deepest moments of faith.

Dr. Newberg says,

"If we're really going to look at this very powerful force in human history of religion and spirituality, I think we really have to take a look at how that affects our brain, what's changing or turning on or turning off, within our brain." The doctor measured brain activity during speaking in tongues to summarize that "what's happening to them neurologically looks a lot like what they report is happening to them spiritually."

The first scan when the person prayed in English showed the frontal lobe, the part of the brain that controls language, was active, but for the most part it fell quiet when they prayed in tongues. Science and faith are not juxtaposed, rather science validates faith. "The gray area where fact meets faith" is the closing line of the segment.[3]

A Power Tool for Every Believer

One winter afternoon as I sat at my work station wondering which task to undertake next, I felt God point out to me that possibly the best work I could do that day was a prayer drive throughout my city. With gratitude for a good heater in my car, I left the office and began to drive slowly up and down one street at a time praying for the people who lived behind the doors of the houses.

I prayed in English and prayed in tongues for needs I knew about and those I had no knowledge of. I cruised through industrial areas, residential areas, and business areas. I stopped in the parking lots of the county library, the public schools, universities, city hall, the police station, the Cleveland Cavaliers' practice facility, hotels, restaurants, and bowling alleys. I talked to God about the needs of our city and listened to His heart about why our church was there and what He hoped would come as a result.

All it cost me was a tank of gas and an afternoon of time to do what I truly believe was the best work I could have done that day. There's no way the experience would have been the same had I prayed from my office. Most significantly, I knew that as I prayed in tongues on my drive through the city I was praying God's will and love for the people in the city.

Leveling the Praying Field

Praying in tongues is also an important aspect of leveling the praying field. It isn't an experience that's limited to a select few but is a gift available for every follower of Christ. The only qualification is to be a believer with spiritual hunger and trust in God. So, when we gather among Christians sharing this belief, let's engage in prayer together and welcome the activity of the Holy Spirit among us.

Questions for Reflection

1 What does the phrase "prayer language" mean to you?

2 Think of a specific time when you gained benefit from praying in tongues. What benefits did you experience?

3 Do you find that your eagerness to pray is attached to your personal feelings or emotions? How much of prayer is just raw discipline or choice?

4 How does a prayer language help us know with certainty that we are praying the will of God?

5 How does praying in tongues help to level the praying field?

7

Spiritual Gifts Fueled by Prayer

"When we persist in prayer, our prayer life progresses from duty to discipline to delight."

—Larry Lea

While I was pastoring at Rockside Church, we did a church-wide survey on a variety of topics. One of the responses that caught the attention of our board and staff was about prayer. When asked, "What is the prayer level of your church?" the results came back with an average of eight out of ten (ten being the highest score). When asked how they would rate their *personal* participation in prayer, the average came back three out of ten. In other words, except for a small group, most attenders felt they were part of a church that was strong in prayer, yet they didn't consider themselves personal contributors to that strength or individually strong in prayer.

To say it another way, "Someone else in this church is pulling my share of responsibility for prayer." To me the results indicated that some participants were probably saying to themselves, *I don't have the gift for praying.* If people think prayer is a gift of the Spirit or an assignment for a few, it would make sense when we are told that a church is beating the norm if more than 10 percent of those who attend come out for a weekly prayer service or any type of prayer meeting.

> Prayer is a choice, a discipline, a decision to talk to God and hear from God, and no one can do your praying for you anymore than someone else can praise or worship for you.

Granted, you'll occasionally find some individuals for whom prayer is a passion and they seem to participate more easily. In reality, prayer is a choice, a discipline, a decision to talk to God and hear from God, and no one can do your praying for you anymore than someone else can praise or worship for you.

Prayer Isn't a Gift of the Spirit

Prayer is a gift of sorts in that we need not pay for the privilege to pray; it's available to everyone equally and it blesses freely. Yet, when we think of the gifts of the Spirit in the Bible, prayer is not one of them.

The gifts of the Spirit named in 1 Corinthians 12:1–11 are just as much for believers today as they were for the first-century church and the disciples.

> **Now about the gifts of the Spirit, brothers and sisters, I do not want you to be uninformed. You know that when you were pagans, somehow or other you were influenced and led astray to mute idols. Therefore I want you to know that no one who is speaking by the Spirit of God says, "Jesus be cursed," and no one can say, "Jesus is Lord," except by the Holy Spirit.**

There are different kinds of gifts, but the same Spirit distributes them. There are different kinds of service, but the same Lord. There are different kinds of working, but in all of them and in everyone it is the same God at work.

Now to each one the manifestation of the Spirit is given for the common good. To one there is given through the Spirit a message of wisdom, to another a message of knowledge by means of the same Spirit, to another faith by the same Spirit, to another gifts of healing by that one Spirit, to another miraculous powers, to another prophecy, to another distinguishing between spirits, to another speaking in different kinds of tongues, and to still another the interpretation of tongues. All these are the work of one and the same Spirit, and he distributes them to each one, just as he determines.

All the gifts are supernatural and designed to become a natural part of life for the follower of Christ. None of the nine gifts is called the "gift of prayer," yet all nine gifts must be fueled by prayer. Each gift is unique and given by the same Spirit. The purpose of the gifts is for the common good of all believers. Notice how this passage continues

> **All the gifts have the common need to be fueled and guided by prayer.**

to toggle back and forth making clear the "sameness" of God while defining the uniqueness of each gift.

Different kinds of gifts   the same Spirit

Different kinds of service   the same Lord

Different kinds of working   the same God

All the gifts have the common need to be fueled and guided by prayer. Distributed as the Spirit of God sees fit, any of the nine gifts is for a person to use, not to keep, claim, or call their own. God distributes them for the good of all believers; the person receiving the gift is simply the vessel or broker of God's blessings to His church. Prayer is the unwritten tool of communication in this passage for every believer to use now and forever to stay in touch with the Giver of gifts, God.

To each one	as He determines
Each one	for the common good
To one	through the Spirit
To another	by means of the same Spirit
To another	by the same Spirit
To another	by that one Spirit
Still another	the work of one and the same Spirit
To each one	as He determines

Why does it matter that we understand prayer isn't one of the gifts? If we regard prayer as something only a few are gifted at, we'll tend to dismiss our involvement in prayer or expect someone else to do our praying for us. We perceive that it comes more easily for some so we conclude they surely must have a gift for prayer. I've heard people say things like, "Dad does the praying for our family" or "Thank God we have a praying grandma," as if to suggest it's an assignment for a few on behalf of everyone else.

While prayer is not one of the gifts of the Spirit, it is the vital communication link between the person used in the gifts and God who is the Giver of the gifts. Prayer directs the gifts to be used well to bring good to all. It keeps the focus on the relationship with the *Giver* instead of on the *gift*.

> While prayer is not one of the gifts of the Spirit, it is the vital communication link between the person used in the gifts and God who is the Giver of the gifts.

If a person is being used in one or more of these gifts but neglects to pray, this can become problematic. In the absence of prayer, pride can set in, and the gift can become the focus instead of the Giver of the gift; the gift can be misused, and instead of helping the church it can even harm the church.

Prayer is the communication tool that keeps the person being used in one of the gifts in a life-giving relationship with the Giver of the gift. The more God uses you in the gifts of the Spirit, the more you need to pray. If you want to be used in one of the gifts of the Spirit, pray. If you want the gifts of the Spirit to operate in your church and among your friends, ask God in prayer.

The Gifts Function Best with Prayer

Let's look more closely at the gifts to see how they function best with prayer (1 Corinthians 12:4–11). We can organize the nine gifts mentioned in this passage into three categories of revelation gifts, power gifts, and utterance gifts.

Revelation Gifts

- A message of wisdom (v. 8)
- A message of knowledge (v. 8)
- Distinguishing between spirits (v. 10)

For the revelation gifts, what we ask for in

prayer is wisdom, knowledge, and discernment. Often, when we have quieted ourselves in prayer to hear God's voice, He will drop into our minds some insight of wisdom, knowledge, or discernment. These gifts function well in the context of prayer.

Power Gifts

- Faith (v. 9)
- Gifts of healing (v. 9)
- Miraculous powers (v. 10)

The power gifts fit perfectly with prayer. When someone needs to be healed, we pray for them. When a miracle takes place, it's usually in response to prayer. And God gives us the gift of faith to power our prayer lives and to believe Him for something beyond our normal level of faith.

Utterance Gifts

- Prophecy (v. 10)
- Tongues (v. 10)
- Interpretation of tongues (v. 10)

The most natural way I've seen the supernatural gift of prophecy work is in the context of praying for someone. Often, something that is said in prayer has been a foretelling or a forthtelling of what God wanted that person to know.

So, you see, prayer is not a gift, but all the gifts are fueled by prayer and often expressed in the context of the act of prayer.

> **Prayer is not a gift, but all the gifts are fueled by prayer and often expressed in the context of the act of prayer.**

Motivational Gifts

Let's look at another set of gifts recorded in Romans 12:6–8 that are often referred to as the motivational gifts. As you will see from the list below, prayer is not mentioned as one of these gifts, but prayer fuels them.

> **We have different gifts, according to the grace given to each of us. If your gift is prophesying, then prophesy in accordance with your faith; if it is serving,**

then serve; if it is teaching, then teach; if it is to encourage, then give encouragement; if it is giving, then give generously; if it is to lead, do it diligently; if it is to show mercy, do it cheerfully.

- Prophesying (prophecy, words)
- Serving (helps, a "worker bee")
- Teaching
- Encouraging (exhortation)
- Giving (contributing)
- Leading (leadership, administration)
- Showing mercy

There is such spiritual satisfaction and richness in functioning in one of these gifts when the gift is saturated in prayer and God is glorified. Be reminded that the Giver of the gift is God, the vessel is you, and the beneficiary of the gift is the community of believers for the glory of God. Without consistent communication between a gifted person and God, it is possible for the gift to flow in the flesh, in a secular context, cutting God out of the mix. But when the gifts are saturated in prayer, they will function at His direction for His glory to the end of benefiting His children who are pursuing His purposes. All the gifts are pulled into the spiritual arena and ongoing prayer makes the difference.

Ministry Gifts

Let's look at one last group of gifts in Ephesians 4. With this group it is easy to identify the why behind the what. Some might think God's gifts are given to make us feel valued, or to prove God exists, or to endorse our personal spirituality. The reason for God's gifts is clear in Ephesians 4:11–16:

> **So Christ himself gave the apostles, the prophets, the evangelists, the pastors and teachers, to equip his people for works of service, so that the body of Christ may be built up until we all reach unity in the faith and in the knowledge**

of the Son of God and become mature, attaining to the whole measure of the fullness of Christ.

Then we will no longer be infants, tossed back and forth by the waves, and blown here and there by every wind of teaching and by the cunning and craftiness of people in their deceitful scheming. Instead, speaking the truth in love, we will grow to become in every respect the mature body of him who is the head, that is, Christ. From him the whole body, joined and held together by every supporting ligament, grows and builds itself up in love, as each part does its work.

The purpose of the gifts is to help us grow up spiritually. Rather than remaining spiritual infants, unstable in our walk with Christ, God wants us to "become mature, attaining to the whole measure of the fullness of Christ" (verse 13).

How does God see that happening? Well, He plans to equip us for works of service. Why? He equips us so the body of Christ may be built up (v. 12). Who is He going to use to do that? He'll use people who are gifts to the church: apostles, prophets, evangelists, pastors, and teachers.

These are known as the fivefold ministry gifts. But what do they have to do with prayer? Note that prayer is, once again, absent from the list of roles affixed to people as gifts to the church. There is no sixth gift titled intercessor or prayer warrior. Rather, all five ministry gifts should flow through a prayerful person for whom others are praying. Imagine these gifted leaders never practicing prayer. Imagine if no one prayed for pastors, teachers, evangelists, prophets, and apostles. Each of the people demonstrating these gifts needs to be covered in prayer by all believers.

Applying Prayer to the Spiritual Gifts

Let's consider some ways we might apply prayer to all the gifts named in the Bible:

1. **Pray that each gift will be used properly.**

We know it is possible to use the gifts improperly because the Bible gives correction to the first-century church on the use of the gifts. Paul wrote letters to the Corinthians, in part, to correct and direct the gifts in the church. The Corinthians were misusing their spiritual gifts and instead of building up the church, they were harming the church (1 Corinthians 3:3, 16–17).

The Bible teaches us how to use the gifts properly. For example, Romans 12:6–8 describes how a person should use their gift:

- If a person's gift is contributing to the needs of others, they are to "give generously."
- If a person's gift is leadership, they should govern "diligently."
- If a person is gifted to show mercy, they should "do it cheerfully."

Clearly there is a right and wrong way to use the gifts. Let us pray that God will help us to use them properly.

2. Pray for the gifts to operate in your life.

The Bible tells us to earnestly desire spiritual gifts (1 Corinthians 14:1) and to "stir up the gift of God which is in you" (2 Timothy 1:6, NKJV). Do you pray for God to use you in these gifts? He wants you to ask Him.

3. Pray for the gifts to be identified and operate correctly in others.

If the gifts bless the whole church and God gives them to whom He chooses, then it benefits all of us to pray that others (as well as ourselves) will receive and use the gifts.

4. Pray that God will be glorified by the gifts.

Possibly the most notable miracle of all is when we humans can get our egos out of the way so God can use us, yet we don't touch His glory. That requires prayer.

5. Pray for God to guide you in using the gifts.

Although God gives the gifts by the Holy Spirit, as individual believers we use the gifts. It is our responsibility to steward the gifts, practice the gifts, unselfishly make our gift available, and use it with humility and grace. We can do that only with God's help.

6. Pray for the creative release of additional gifts.

Consider that the gifts God gives are not limited to those named specifically in the Bible. Perhaps the lists we have in the Bible are just starter lists. I've met people who, to the glory of God, were gifted with the ability to clean out a closet and organize space, crunch numbers, cook, care for the elderly, paint, program computers, or change diapers. The Bible says that "Every good and perfect gift is from above, coming down from the Father of the heavenly lights, who does not change like shifting shadows" (James 1:17). What other gifts might you use to bring glory to God? Pray for them!

Take prayer away from the gifts and what is the result? The gifts remain dormant on the shelf, are used in a wrong or even harmful way, and do not benefit the body of Christ. Without prayer, the person using the gift can take the credit, have the wrong attitude or faulty theology, even become tired and resent the gift. Take prayer away, and the gift becomes the focus instead of the Giver of the gift. Take prayer away, and the church believes the gifts are no longer necessary or relevant for the body of Christ.

Prayer is not one of the spiritual gifts. Rather, it is a gift God has given His children to talk to Him and hear from Him and to build up the body of Christ.

Questions for Reflection

1 What comes to your mind when people seem to identify themselves as a "prayer specialist"? How is this not a biblical idea?

2 What gifts has God given to you? How does prayer help you operate in the gifts?

3 How does prayer support the way we use spiritual gifts?

4 How might you want to pray about the topic of spiritual gifts for your church?

5 How does prayer keep the gifts operating in a biblical manner?

8

Building an On-Ramp to Prayer

"The truth about prayer is that God the Sovereign Lord invites us into a privileged place of partnership with Him."

—William Philip

A team from our church was returning to the United States after an adventurous missions trip to Bogota, Colombia. Our plane had just taken off from Colombia and leveled out in the air when all the oxygen masks abruptly dropped from overhead, dangling in our faces. We've all heard the drill from the airline staff so many times we tune it out, but now it was our reality. It was time to draw on the memory of those rote instructions to see if we knew what to do.

The captain's voice pierced the gasps, chattering, and chaos. "Ladies and gentlemen, we're losing cabin pressure in the plane. Please place the oxygen masks over your nose and mouth. Pull the string snuggly and breathe normally even if the bag doesn't inflate. Please put on your own mask first before attempting to help those around you. We are returning the plane to the Bogota airport."

It seemed like the trip back to the airport was at least twice as far as the distance we had already traveled. I would guess the next moments caused most passengers to pray with whatever understanding they had of prayer. In moments like this, we grab on to prayer the best way we know how, whether it's the Lord's Prayer, a made-up prayer, or repeating the name of Jesus. There's no wrong way to pray when the main appeal is, "Help us, Lord!" Everyone can and does pray. The praying field suddenly becomes level.

Eventually we learned that the reason emergency vehicles with flashing lights awaited us on the runway included the additional problem that the landing gear would not lower, and the plane was full—full of passengers, luggage and cargo, and unused fuel since we were at the start of the trip.

After we landed safely, the pilot acknowledged what a miracle we had experienced with words familiar to him, "Someone above was looking out for us because we just experienced a miracle." We deplaned, eventually boarded a different plane, and returned home with pictures and a story to tell of God's miraculous help.

I thought back to that flight recently when I read a post on Facebook that included a quote from an article I had written: "Have you breathed today? Prayer is to the Christian what breathing is to the body." Each person must pray regularly on their own. Others can't do it for us.

Most of what I've learned about prayer has

been from looking over the shoulder of admired mentors while they prayed. The best way to help others pray is do it and bring them along with you.

Help Others with Their "Oxygen" Supply

My guess is you wouldn't be reading this book if you didn't already have a passion, or at least an appreciation, for prayer. So, here's the challenge. Look around and ask God to identify a few people whom you can mentor in the area of prayer and bring them out of the stands and onto the praying field with you. Look around the prayer plane to see who doesn't have their "oxygen mask" on and reach out to help them.

> Most of what I've learned about prayer has been from looking over the shoulder of admired mentors while they prayed.

A baby gets its oxygen supply from the mother until he or she is born. Then the cord is snipped, and the baby must breathe on his or her own. The

Coaching for Pastors

Even while I'm writing this book on prayer, I'm continually being challenged and reminded that this can't take the place of my own personal time of prayer. As vocational ministers or pastors, it's normal for us to talk about prayer, read books on prayer, teach on it, mention it in sermons, tell people we're praying for them, read about prayer in the Bible, truly believe in prayer . . . all the while our own "oxygen mask" of prayer has slipped out of position, and it's been a while since we've taken in a deep breath of prayer for ourselves.

There's no substitute for personally participating in prayer for ourselves. Before we can ever be of help to someone else, we first must be breathing in and breathing out this conversation with God called prayer.

same is true of prayer. We can't relegate prayer to a handful of "specialists" and rely on them to breathe for us. What if only a few passengers on that plane had put on the oxygen masks and told the rest of the passengers, "Don't worry, we'll do your breathing for you!" Why, it would only be a matter of minutes until bodies would have collapsed all over the floor of that plane. It would be ridiculous and fatal, right? If we saw a fellow passenger to our left or right without their oxygen mask in place, we wouldn't think twice about doing whatever we could to assist them.

Likewise, each of us, after embracing our own prayer involvement, must look around and see what God might want us to do to help others include a life-giving supply of prayer in their lives. That's how most of us got started on this journey of following Christ, by praying. Whether we called it a "sinner's prayer" or a "salvation prayer" or a prayer of desperation that simply said, "God if You're there, please help me!" prayer was the beginning. But it's a beginning meant to continue every step of the way, one breath at a time.

God wants all His children to talk with Him and listen to Him. When He created Adam and Eve, it was His joy to walk with them in the cool of the day and to talk with them. That's still His desire. We please the Father's heart when we talk and listen to Him and when we bring others to the conversation as well.

Mentoring Others in Prayer

Whether you're a pastor, a parent, or a Christian wanting to multiply yourself as a praying disciple of Christ, let's think about ways you can mentor others in prayer. Think about the prayer meeting you attend or the prayer commitments that are on your calendar. What if the "win" was not how long a few of us prayed, but rather how many new participants found their way into the experience by our encouragement? If you're already strong in your prayer life, if you're a positive participant in group prayer efforts, the challenge for you is to consider what it would take to encourage someone who's not strong in those areas to come participate with you.

> God wants all His children to talk with Him and listen to Him.

Think about the gradual on-ramp to an interstate highway. It's built with a curve that's possible to manage and won't throw your car into the field. The ramp has a grade that lets drivers from a side road access the interstate easily. There's enough distance on the ramp so you can accelerate and get into the flow of the rest of the traffic gradually and safely.

So what kind of "on-ramp" can you create to help others find success in praying? How can you help them move forward a few notches from where they are and grow as a participant rather than just listening to others pray or not be present at all? Sometimes it's as simple as modeling for them a way to pray that causes them to think, *I could probably do that.*

Sometimes it's just being mindful to stop what may be a deterrent to others from joining in. Sometimes it's something simply stylistic: a person prays using a different voice than they normally talk with. Or they use religious jargon that is unfamiliar. Or they pray extremely long prayers and the novice at prayer might think, *Oh, I could never pray like that.* They might even compliment that person on how well they pray. But that's not the goal. The sign of a successful prayer time is when we've helped others grow in their willingness to talk to God and hear from God for themselves, especially if they're just learning to pray or have limited experience in prayer.

Here are some other ideas about ways you might include others in times of prayer and encourage them to participate.

Home: Among those who live with you, it begins with prayer at junctures such as mealtime, bedtime, or when leaving the home at the top of the day. When praying with or for them, let your prayer set an example by being an accessible length and made of words everyone knows. Ask others to pray and encourage them on a job well done. Make home a safe place to pray where nothing in a prayer is used

> The sign of a successful prayer time is when we've helped others grow in their willingness to talk to God and hear from God for themselves, especially if they're just learning to pray or have limited experience in prayer.

against others, and where no one is scolded for the style or length or content of their prayer.

Daily Opportunities: Natural opportunities for prayer often surface when it doesn't feel weird to suggest a brief prayer, but is normal in the setting or circumstances. For example:

- The neighbor mentions he's going in for surgery tomorrow.
- The car is loaded and you're ready to depart on a long road trip and want to ask for God's protection.
- The kids or grandkids are being tucked into bed for the night.
- You're taking a housewarming gift to a friend who has a new home that needs to be prayed over.
- A colleague is taking a big exam tomorrow.
- The Uber driver shares with you his marriage is breaking up and the kids are fearful.
- Your niece has been offered a job in another city but isn't sure if she should accept it.

Without making anyone uncomfortable or being socially awkward, there are natural opportunities like these that God will guide you to use for on-ramps of prayer, even with pre-Christians. Here's the key: Make it a great experience for the other person! That might mean being sensitive to brevity, volume, who else is around, or whether you touch them or not. It's a great opportunity for others to observe how natural and normal it is to include communication with God in the everyday events of life. Hopefully, this will encourage them to do the same.

> **When you're alert and watching for these opportunities, you can step into them quickly, say the prayer naturally, and move on.**

When you're alert and watching for these opportunities, you can step into them quickly, say the prayer naturally, and move on. It just becomes as easy as Jesus being an unseen guest with you whom you introduce, include, and keep moving. Nothing weird, just naturally including your supernatural Friend in the natural interaction.

Spiritual Responsibility: As parents, you are the primary Christian educators of your children. In the Jewish culture, children were spiritually trained at home and gathered at the temple to hear the Torah read. Thank God for children's spiritual training at church, but the first line of responsibility rests in the home. It's not an option, but your God-given responsibility to model, teach, assist, and affirm active prayer in your home. With children and teens, sometimes it's as simple as having a habit of prayer at mealtimes and asking one of them to say the prayer. Agree with them by saying, "Amen" at the end and don't make it a big deal that could embarrass them or create comparisons among the other kids. Just pass the potatoes and move on.

Coaching for Pastors

If you're a spiritual leader of others (teacher, group leader, pastor, etc.), help those in your group to find an on-ramp for prayer. Even as a colleague to others in a church, every person in that church is a candidate to be mentored toward prayerfulness.

Sometimes including others in a prayer effort is as simple as scheduling a time of prayer and planning for it. Consider how you can design the prayer time in a way that will attract and include people who might not otherwise attend.

Leading a prayer meeting might be one of the most labor intensive, most difficult tasks a pastor will ever face, and there is often minimal training provided for that task. I had a clergy friend tell me once, "To be honest, I don't really know how to lead a prayer meeting." What if you gave as much creative preparation to prayer meetings as to any other task on your plate? If you're a leader in any capacity among the people who attend your church, think about ways you can incorporate and increase partici-patory prayer among those you serve.

Providing an On-Ramp for
People of Other Faiths

When three people died of opioid overdose in one week in the city where our church was located, a city leader called me and asked if I would organize and conduct a prayer meeting. They knew prayer was needed but couldn't spearhead it in their roles and didn't feel equipped. What an honor! I can tell you that invitation rose to the top of my priority list. I was ready to move whatever I needed to off my schedule to make room for this. I mean, a pastor can wait a lifetime for a call like that, right? And what do we have on our to-do list as spiritual shepherds that could possibly be more important than helping people in the community talk to God and hear from God?

First we reserved the Old Town Hall, promoted the date and time, and put some plans in place. Knowing our city was 73 percent Roman Catholic and knowing their style of prayer was to read a prepared prayer, we created handouts with a few written prayers. Then we selected pertinent topics and Scriptures, and invited people to lead in prayer around a given theme. Several people, most of them from our church, led in prayer. We concluded by reciting the Lord's Prayer together, which works well for most Christian circles, whether Roman Catholic or Protestant. As we were visiting with one another and saying our good-byes, a Catholic woman said, "I wonder if we could ask Father Pete to teach us to pray like some of you prayed . . . you know, making up your own prayers to God instead of reading them."

That captured my heart and my attention. I realized we had found common ground—to talk to God and hear from God around a crisis in our city—that helped us all to mature in our prayer lives and unite together. Prayer is such a unifier if we will dodge the barriers and seek to include rather than stand apart. As I coached our people before we arrived, I asked them to be mindful to pray short prayers that included others and didn't sound pompous and polished. Their prayers should sound like they were talking to God with and on behalf of the group rather than having the group listen in while they talked to God. That can be as simple as, "Lord, we need and we ask" as opposed to "Lord, I ask." The goal was to create gradual on-ramps for all who attended so everyone could participate at some level and feel comfortably included and capable of joining in. No one wants to feel "not good" at anything, so why not set them up to succeed!

When I hosted my Hindu neighbor for lunch or was a guest in her home, it was my custom from the start of our friendship to say, "I like to pray to Jesus over my meal. Would you mind if I said a short prayer for us?" Before long the pattern was established, and she would pause, expecting me to pray before we ate. When we were in her home to eat, she even asked me to pray. Over time, I asked her, "Would you like to pray, or would you like me to?" My friend would chuckle and tell me to pray. One day she surprised me when I asked that question. This time her response was, "Sure, I will give it a try." She prayed to Jesus the most beautiful prayer that made my heart swell with joy. She was no longer observing, but was talking to Jesus in prayer!

Leveling the Praying Field

Help those under your care find an on-ramp. Assist those around you with their oxygen masks! Mentor others in prayer. You can do this!

Questions for Reflection

1 What have you seen people do in prayer that caused others to have an uncomfortable experience? How could this have been avoided?

2 What have others done to mentor you in prayer?

3 What recent situations in your normal course of life have caused you to pause in prayer?

4 What people in your life need your leadership in learning to pray? How can you reach out to them?

5 How might thinking about Jesus instead of thinking about themselves give people confidence to pray?

9

Helping Others Participate in Prayer

"Converting our unceasing think-ing into unceasing prayer move us from a self-centered monologue to a God-centered dialogue."

—Henri Nouwen

I have always been intrigued by the report in the Bible when Jesus got ticked off. Maybe it wasn't the only time He got angry, but this is the scene that appears in the Bible. There are so many aspects to it. One version reports that before unleashing His wrath, Jesus took time to weave a whip, suggesting the absence of an impulsive outburst but rather intentional deliberation (John 2:15). He turned over the tables and physically chased the money changers and their birds and animals out of the temple, which adds such drama and passion to the scene.

> **On reaching Jerusalem, Jesus entered the temple courts and began driving out those who were buying and selling there. He overturned the tables of the money changers and the benches of those selling doves and would not allow anyone to carry merchandise through the temple courts. And as he taught them, he said, "Is it not written: 'My house will be called a house of prayer for all nations'? But you have made it 'a den of robbers'"** (Mark 11:15–17).

Jesus' spoken words at the scene are quoted from the Old Testament, bringing clout beyond what His audience might have had the knowledge to give Him under the circumstances. It was also language appropriate for the location. His words suggest He was indignant on behalf of His Heavenly Father. Continuously an advocate for the marginalized, Jesus' love for justice couldn't bear to see the cheating scams taking place before His eyes. As people arrived at the entrance of the temple, the way should have been easy for them to meet with God. Instead, money changers were taking advantage of them with deceitful financial gouging in the name of God. You can feel Jesus' rage, can't you? And then He shouted those famous words, "Is it not written, 'My house shall be called a house of prayer for all nations'? But you have made it a 'den of thieves'" (Mark 11:17, NKJV).

As a pastor, I often used that phrase as a reminder that of all the things a local church could give itself to, Jesus wants it to be a "house of prayer." I also used it as a springboard for prayer for our missionaries serving around the world and their country: "We are a house of prayer, not just for our own city, but for the nations. It was Jesus who said, 'My house will be called a house of prayer for all nations.'"

In the process of writing this book, my friend Dr. Carolyn Tennant challenged me in a brief but powerful chat to burrow deeper into this passage. Could it be that what angered Jesus most was that everyone was not equally welcome to the place of the presence of God? Jesus wanted every person, without prejudice, to have access to God's presence, a leveling of the praying field so to speak, and that was not happening! The economic divide kept out some who couldn't afford to buy the overpriced offerings. The ethnic divide allowed Jews to enter beyond where Gentiles were permitted. The physical clutter of the tables and commerce distracted and blocked access

> Jesus wanted every person, without prejudice, to have access to God's presence, a leveling of the praying field.

for others. Jesus' heart burned with the priority of His Heavenly Father: that this holy space to meet with God should have no obstacles and no prejudice. In that moment of capturing everyone's attention, it was Jesus' heartfelt passion to level the praying field. He wanted the house of God to be a house of prayer accessible to all people.

Praying with Others

Some people who are uncomfortable praying alongside others might ask, "Do I have to pray with others for God to hear my prayer?" Of course, the answer is an unequivocal no. Jesus often sought a place to be alone when He prayed. I love Mark 1:35 (NLT), "Before daybreak the next morning, Jesus got up and went out to an isolated place to pray."

There are often reasons and seasons when it simply isn't feasible for us to pray with others. However, God's Word encourages us to pray with other believers. "Where two or three are gathered together in My name, I am there in the midst of them" (Matthew 18:20, NKJV). The disciples went to the temple at specific times daily for prayer and Scripture reading, and corporate prayer is mentioned throughout the Bible. If Jesus said God's house would be a house of prayer for the nations, He was probably referring to corporate prayer, otherwise everyone could have prayed at home.

So, what does it look like when we come together in prayer? I recently heard a comment at a church gathering that went something like, "That guy is able to go on and on in prayer, so we just let him pray and the rest of us watch." We chuckle about that, but unfortunately sometimes that's what a corporate prayer time becomes rather than everyone finding an on-ramp of participation.

How do we pray together? When we come together in prayer, there's a corporate expression among the group if we flow in that. So, we listen as another person prays and we agree with them; we are provoked, inspired, burdened, and encouraged. Then we watch and listen for what God is saying and how He is directing the group.

Where is this prayer time flowing? What is God saying to me through my fellow believers? How does God want to use me to be His voice to others? How is our agreement in prayer moving heaven? What Scriptures could guide this time of prayer? That is the essence of corporate prayer, and it's wonderful when we find the flow of it and help others to participate.

Find creative on-ramps, ways to include every person there in the conversation of prayer with God.

This is the time to notice whether some are finding it difficult to participate with the group and help them out. How might you begin reaching out to help them become comfortable in that setting?

Have you ever been with someone who bumped into an old friend and the two of them started visiting while you waited to be introduced? The more the two who knew each other visited and time passed, the more awkward you felt standing there. You started to think that perhaps you should just walk away and let them visit as you feel more invisible. That same kind of excluding can happen in a prayer meeting. Rather than seeing one person do all the praying on behalf of others, think in terms of finding creative on-ramps, ways to include every person there in the conversation of prayer with God. What a beautiful thing when a person new to a prayer meeting feels included in the conversation and senses that they, too, are talking to God and hearing from God rather than merely observing others do this.

> A good way to help people feel comfortable with corporate prayer is to provide prayer events they can participate in.

Encouraging People
to Participate in Prayer

For a local pastor, creating prayer events can require more creativity and planning than any other part of your work. However, it has the best "return on investment." A good way to help people feel comfortable with corporate prayer is to provide prayer events they can participate in. Why not plan a trip into your community to pray for needs on-site? When a smaller group of believers meet for prayer in an off-site casual setting, those who participate get to know one another on a more personal level, which helps break down barriers of praying in public. We regularly planned events like this at Rockside Church.

For example, Cherie arranged for us to meet in her kindergarten classroom at an inner-city Cleveland school where issues ranged from underfunding, violence, students who were homeless or lived with a grandparent, and insufficient classroom aids. We prayed for Cherie, her colleagues, and her students. It touched me deeply to drive through the neighborhood of poverty that is her trip every morning, walk the halls of her building, sit in the kiddy chairs of her classroom, and see the students' papers on the bulletin board. It helped all of us understand Cherie's daily world as a representative of Christ in such a desperate and challenging environment, where many of her students find it difficult to focus on their studies because they are hungry. Cherie invited us to step right into the deepest needs of her daily world and fill it with prayer.

Could we have prayed for her from the sanctuary just the same? We certainly could have prayed for her in the church, but I have no doubt the intensity of our prayers and the lasting effects would have been entirely different. Taking a group of praying believers into that setting left an invisible imprint on us to continue to pray for our city's students and educators with empathy.

As a result of that visit, our church adopted that school and began to help in practical ways through Cherie as our liaison by buying supplies and aids for the students and providing classroom volunteers. That group of praying friends also left a snapshot in Cherie's memory that reminded her on the most challenging days that she was not alone—her classroom was holy ground and God was with her.

Another helpful way to get everyone involved in corporate prayer is to create prayer events that are a bit out of the box.

Scott and John are brothers and over-the-road truck drivers in our congregation. Wanting in on the "pray where you work" focus our congregation was following, we arranged for them to bring their eighteen-wheelers to church on a specific Sunday. At the end of service, the entire congregation joined together in the parking lot for prayer. I asked John and Scott, in their booming voices, to tell us how we could pray for the trucking industry and for their families.

> Another helpful way to get everyone involved in corporate prayer is to create prayer events that are a bit out of the box.

They shared what a challenge it was for them to be out of town Monday through Friday with only forty-eight hours at home on the weekends. In that short time, they had to manage household chores, car repairs, birthday parties, and church attendance. They also shared the dangers of being out on the highway, the temptations and

evils of the culture of truck-stop life, the discom-
fort of sleeping in their trucks, and their desire for
God to send them ministry opportunities during
the workweek. We got a glimpse of what their
work environment was like and learned how we
could pray for them.

We made a huge circle around their trucks
and prayed. Then we walked around their trucks,
laying our hands on
the trucks and pray-
ing. On the dashboard
of his truck, Scott
had several "sermon
reminders" we had
passed out over time
that he kept as handy
reminders. The kids

> It has always been my goal to help the people I minister to each week interact in prayer with believers from other churches and walks of life.

really enjoyed climbing into the cabs of the trucks
and getting a chance to sound the horns.

This was such a fun and relaxed way to minister
to the needs of Scott and John. At the same time,

our congregation bonded together, and everyone experienced the power of prayer. People who trembled at the thought of praying in public felt confident enough to pray a few words out there in the parking lot. It was a great first step for many of them.

Praying with People from Other Tribes in the Body of Christ

It has always been my goal to help the people I minister to each week interact in prayer with believers from other churches and walks of life. One of the most basic ways to initiate something like this is to plan an event for the National Day of Prayer. It's always the first Thursday of May, and the website (www.nationaldayofprayer.org) provides abundant resources, information, and a place to post and retrieve information about prayer sites.

The first year Rockside Church opened, the core group met for leader development on Friday nights although we had not yet begun Sunday services and were not open to the public. We were engaged in community outreach, so on the National Day of Prayer we decided to host a prayer hour at noon in the small auditorium of a local office building. We posted fliers around the area and did some advertising with the Chamber of Commerce. Our core group members provided music, and various ones led in prayer. About fifty people joined us that first time.

It was a simple beginning, but year after year it grew and grew. The next year we hosted a Day of Prayer event in our church sanctuary at noon. Then we moved it to 7:00 p.m. and changed the location to the middle school auditorium. Each year we met a few days later to evaluate the prayer time and discuss how we could improve it the next year. The group who participated in planning the event grew to include the city's clerk of courts, the mayor's assistant, the spiritual director from the local Kiwanis Club, and a few other members of the clergy in the city. It was a turning point for us when we realized the attendees were typical and the venue had created a silo effect. So it was time for a change.

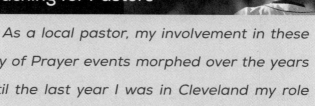

As a local pastor, my involvement in these Day of Prayer events morphed over the years until the last year I was in Cleveland my role was more of a distant organizer and encourager. Each of the prayer stations had a leader much more suited to the audience and purpose.

For example, instead of a pastor leading prayer with the students, it was a Campus Life director. The chief of police led prayer where firetrucks and police cars pulled up. Public servants in uniform and veterans gathered around the memorial in the center of town to pray for men and women in uniform. A mental health professional led prayer at the local counseling center. A believer who is a businessman led the prayer segment in his office building for the business community. The students in St. Michael's School took the lead and presented an excellent prayer service in their sanctuary. The city provided a brunch in the civic center where people gathered around tables and volunteers guided them to participate in prayer.

God was redirecting us to go outside the walls of our church to where the people were and find a way to engage people in prayer who might not typically come to a prayer meeting in a church. So the next year, the group had the idea to host prayer stations at strategic locations through the city. We would plan them at various times throughout the day so that everyone who wanted to could find a spot on the clock that worked for them. We would invite people to lead the stations that would attract attendees because of who was leading the segment. Year after year the momentum built for this event. We continually adjusted our tactics and adapted to improve, publicizing the various stations with posters, fliers, billboards, and e-blasts.

When we bought an ad in the local newspaper, the publisher asked me to write an article about the National Day of Prayer events, which tells the story best:

National Day of Prayer—
a Smorgasbord of Choices!

By DONNA BARRETT

Whether it's sandwich toppings at Subway or options at the Starbucks' counter, we are a culture accustomed to options and having it our way. In its 15th year of participation in the city of Independence, our involvement in the NATIONAL DAY OF PRAYER is likewise peppered with choices.

On May 3, 2018, always the first Thursday of May since President Harry Truman signed the bill in 1952, the website www.nationaldayofprayer.org provides resources, ideas, history, promo videos, and a place to enter a zip code to locate the prayer event nearest you across our nation.

Some of the best leaders of prayer in Independence are young people. Students from St. Michael's School actually lead the prayer service at 12:50 p.m. in St. Michael's Church sanctuary, which is open to the public regardless of faith. Students will gather around the flagpole between the Independence middle school and high school at 7:00 a.m. led by Ashley Tengler, director of Campus Life.

We've all seen signs recently saying "More Than Thoughts & Prayers." That is true. The Bible says to pray and take action. We need both! An example of both prayer and action is the good folks at Cornerstone of Hope who provide professional counseling for hundreds annually. They also know the value of prayer and will host the 10:00 a.m. prayer segment at 5905 Brecksville Road led by Ty Morgan.

People will begin gathering before 11:00 a.m. in the White Oak Room of the Civic Center around tables of nourishment: spiritual nourishment as clergy from our churches lead in prayer followed by physical nourishment as lunch is served. There is no charge, but RSVP must be called in to (555) 524–7373 by 4.27.18.

Your eyes just may tear up as men and women in uniform (police, firefighters, and veterans) walk across the grass to the Veterans' Memorial on Brecksville Road. Who better to lead that 5:30 p.m. segment this year than our city's police chief, Michael Kilbane.

The business community is such an integral part of our city and certainly in need of prayer. Businessman Lawrence Liptak will lead the 2:00 p.m. prayer segment in his company's office building, All Crane Rental, 4700 Acorn Drive, off Oak Tree Blvd.

What's different this year is that the 7:00 p.m. gathering will take place at the Concordia Lutheran Church, 6705 Brecksville Road, led by Rev. Robert Hendrix.

Serving as a reminder to the entire city to stop and PRAY, the bells of area churches will ring at the noon hour. Every segment is free and open to the public. The full schedule is available by logging on to www.rocksidechurch.com or check the ad in this issue.

So which spot in Independence will you choose? Maybe your choice is based on the time of day, the location, the leader, or the theme. The choice is yours and starts with the great choice to simply participate! Prayer does make a difference!

Leveling the Praying Field

Prayer is a great unifier. It unified people within our church as they helped make it happen and participate. It unified people in the city regardless of denomination. We couldn't have accomplished any of it without dedicated men and women from our church and the community who shared our goal of involving a broad spectrum of the community in prayer.

What better center-point could a community gather around than prayer? It's immeasurable what happens in the heavenlies when a city prays together. I have no doubt that our Heavenly Father was pleased to see thousands of people finding an on-ramp to participate personally in talking to Him and hearing from Him.

Questions for Reflection

1 How could your church provide an opportunity for those who are not confident in prayer to become comfortable with corporate prayer?

2 Have you ever participated in a prayer event held for people in your church to pray in a setting outside the church? How did that affect you?

3 What types of events could your church plan for corporate prayer in a setting outside the sanctuary?

4 How can you become involved in a National Day of Prayer event?

10

Relational Wisdom and Prayer

"God is great not just because nothing is too big for Him; God is great because nothing is too small for Him."

—Mark Batterson

Years ago, I went to a prayer meeting attended by three other people who discussed in detail the "prayer requests" on their lists for more than ninety minutes (without exaggeration). Then they "wrapped up" the prayer time by asking God to care for those needs. On my way out the door, I thought, *Never again!*

You've likely had similar thoughts about experiences at prayer meetings. Maybe you've asked yourself, *Why is that person screaming into the microphone when they pray?* or *What do those words even mean that I've never heard in my life?* or *How could I ever agree with that person in prayer when they're mumbling so softly I can't hear a word they're saying?*

You could probably add some comical stories about prayer meetings that have sent people running away, determined never to return. Sometimes it's the practical and obvious elements that level the praying field and allow others to engage in the experience. It can be a matter of fine-tuning our focus to the people and prayer practices at hand. Possibly the best grid I've found to drop over a prayer meeting to create an experience and atmosphere that engages everyone present through personal awareness are the principles Ken Sande teaches in his Relational Wisdom 360 material (www.rw360.org).

My favorite definition of relational wisdom is emotional intelligence from a Christian perspective blended with the God factor. Ken Sande identifies relational wisdom as "your ability to discern emotions, interests and abilities in yourself and others, to interpret this information in the light of God's Word, and to use these insights to manage your responses and relationships successfully."[4] He has organized the Bible's teaching on relational wisdom into six core skills grouped into three pairs: (1) how we relate to God; (2) how we relate to ourselves; and (3) how we relate to others. Each of these three skill groups has an "awareness" component (what we see and understand) and an "engaging" component (what we do and say).

When we drop this grid of relational wisdom over prayer, it helps us level the praying field for others to participate. Let's look more closely.

1. **Become self-aware:** In the context of prayer, how can I honestly discern my own interests, values, emotions, strengths, and weaknesses?

2. **Become self-engaged:** In the context of prayer, how can I manage my thoughts, emotions, words, and actions so they advance God's purposes?

3. **Become others-aware:** In the context of prayer, I need God to give me the ability to

understand and empathize with the experiences, emotions, and interests of others.

4. **Become others-engaged:** In the context of prayer, how can I encourage, cooperate, and build bridges with others so they can grow in their participation in prayer?

5. **Become God-aware:** In the context of prayer, how can I tune in to what God wants for this prayer time and what is His will among us?

6. **Become God-engaged:** How can I trust, obey, and engage God in a way that pleases and honors Him and draws others into this time of prayer?[5]

How this plays out is limitless but applying these six skills will help you level the praying field for others, whether you're the pastor leading the prayer meeting or a participant attending the prayer meeting. Now let's look at how Jesus applied these principles when He prayed.

Jesus Applied Relational Wisdom
in His Prayer for Lazarus

When Jesus was at the tomb of Lazarus, He was a great example of practicing relational wisdom. (You can read the entire account of the death and resurrection of Lazarus in John 11.) Let's consider how Jesus did this:

1. Jesus was *others-aware* when He noticed their grief. He was *others-engaged* when He listened, shared, wept, and prayed with the audience in mind: short and loud.

2. Jesus was *self-aware* when He tuned in to His own emotions and outwardly wept! He was *self-engaged* because He wasn't offended when Lazarus's family expressed disappointment that He hadn't arrived sooner.

3. What is most important is how Jesus was tuned in to His Heavenly Father. He was *God-aware* in that He already knew God's intention for that event was a resurrection, not a healing; that God's priority wasn't

Mary's comfort, but God's glory. Jesus was *God-engaged* by praying in advance of His arrival at the home of Mary and Martha, listening to God's timing (not other people's or even His own), and engaging God boldly at the site of the tomb.

What great modeling Jesus provides for us in this powerful scene!

Jesus prayed privately before praying publicly.

Jesus was in ongoing communication with His Heavenly Father about Lazarus even before Jesus arrived on the scene. Thus He was tuned in to the situation and relationally wise in His responses. When you have the opportunity to pray in public, make the effort to become familiar with the situation and with the people involved beforehand if possible. Ask God to make you aware of unseen needs and His purposes for the event and His assignment to you.

Jesus considered the length of His prayer.

Jesus' prayer for Lazarus was just three words: "Lazarus, come out!" (John 11:43). God did His best work (resurrection from the dead) in response to a three-word prayer. Sometimes if our prayer is too long, it can be counterproductive and turn away the hearts of the people we're praying with or it might keep others from having the chance to lead out in prayer. If your "others-awareness" helps you notice a hospital patient is lonely for God's presence, then a longer prayer might be appropriate. On the other hand, if you notice the patient is in pain, maybe a short prayer would be best.

I admired the public prayer Father Pete Colletti prayed at the first tree-lighting Christmas celebration I attended in the city of Independence. The temperature was cold, there were many aspects to the event, and families were struggling to keep their kids supervised. He stepped up to the microphone when called upon and prayed a very loud, cheerful, short prayer. At the time I thought, *How smart of him to be relationally wise, so more people want prayer in their lives!*

Jesus considered the volume of His prayer.

God can hear us whether we whisper or shout our prayer, but when we're praying publicly, volume matters. For example, if you're praying loudly at a table in a restaurant, you might unnecessarily offend other patrons and make your guests feel uncomfortable. If you go with a group to pray for a sick patient, being aware and engaged would not be consistent with shouting down heaven while the patient in the next bed is sleeping or speaking with her doctor.

On the other hand, there can be times when group prayer is too soft. While God can hear even a whispered prayer, it's difficult for other people with us to agree together and participate if they can't hear us. If it's our turn to pray and we bow our head and voice to the floor and mumble, that really disconnects all the others from being a part of the prayer time. If I'm opening a city council meeting with prayer, I'm going to stand and use the microphone to be sure everyone present can hear me. In any public prayer situation, consider carefully the volume and length of your prayer, and

> God can hear us whether we whisper or shout our prayer, but when we're praying publicly, volume matters.

when possible, prepare in advance for that time of prayer.

So, what does it look like to use these six elements of relational wisdom to level the praying field? It's different for us all. For me, for example, my preference is to pray aloud and join in verbally as others pray. But if the person praying is speaking softly, I could become distracting or drown out the person giving the primary prayer. I'm self-aware

> One of the best ways to be others-engaged and others-aware is the act of praying for others.

that praying in my prayer language is distracting or even offensive in some circles, so I try to tune into the setting.

To be others-aware could be as simple as noticing who's comfortable praying aloud and who has never done that. Observe whether there are children or youth in the room and how they might best participate in the prayer time. When people seem hesitant but eager to participate in prayer, provide a bit of instruction and guidance so they know how to join in.

Others-Aware in the Act of Prayer

One of the best ways to be others-engaged and others-aware is the act of praying for others. In effect, we take the hand of a person with one hand and we take the hand of God with the other hand to stand as a bridge of prayer between the two. We can do this any time, any place, and as often as we like. This is how we obey Jesus' timeless command, " 'Love the Lord your God with all your heart' . . . and . . . 'Love your neighbor as yourself' " (Matthew 22:37–39).

So, how do I pray for others? It's pretty simple and I find it helpful to take the mystery out of it. Praying to God on behalf of someone else is asking for God's will for that person. How do we know what that is? We pray in agreement with the Word of God, and we pray knowing that Jesus is at the right hand of the Father to intercede for us (Acts 2:33). "Therefore he is able to save completely those who come to God through him, because he always lives to intercede for them" (Hebrews 7:25). We may not know exactly what to pray for a person, but Jesus does. We can never miss the mark when we pray for God's will to be done.

Leveling the Praying Field

When we pray for others, we intervene or mediate on their behalf to our Heavenly Father. If we want to level the praying field, what better way to start than by standing beside others as a prayer mediator, especially for those who are learning to pray or lack the confidence to pray.

Wouldn't it be wonderful if every time we saw them we could tell them: "I have not stopped giving thanks for you, remembering you in my prayers" (Ephesians 1:16). I can't help but think that this would be ample motivation for them to do the same to others. At that rate, it wouldn't take long to level the praying field!

Questions for Reflection

1 What self-awareness could you engage in that would help others to participate in prayer?

2 During times of corporate prayer, what do you notice about the circumstances and people present that affect how you pray so they can enter in?

3 It may seem ironic that we would not be God-aware and God-engaged about prayer while we are praying. How does that happen and what can we do about it?

4 How can we love others by being a "bridge of prayer" for them?

11

Viewing the Praying Field from the Goodyear Blimp

"Prayers outlive the lives of those who uttered them: outlive a generation, outlive an age, outlive a world."

—E. M. Bounds

You can watch a game on the playing field from the field, from the stands, from the locker room, from the concession stand, or from the parking lot among tailgaters. But, one of the most intriguing views is from the Goodyear Blimp soaring high above the field, with an expanded view from the stadium to the tall buildings of the host city.

That sky-high view reminds me of a view of prayer that goes beyond time into eternity, both past and future. It puts into context the priceless value of prayer, raising it beyond one more self-help pursuit, or even spiritual discipline. It raises prayer to preparation and practice for eternity that brings pleasure to our Creator.

> Talking to God and hearing from Him isn't simply a goal to pursue; it's the breath of every other pursuit!

So, what do you imagine could be the best outcome if you could apply what you've read in this book and what you've processed in the questions for reflection? Think about that. Possibly you'd even like to jot down in the back of this book what that could look like for you.

If this pursuit of prayer and leveling the praying field only become more goals to work on, such as losing ten pounds, decluttering your home, or some other self-help ambition, you have missed out on the higher purpose and full essence of prayer. Talking to God and hearing from Him isn't simply a goal to pursue; it's the breath of every other pursuit! It determines which pursuits get purged and which are worth your attention. It determines how you live your life. To help bring prayer into focus, let's take a glimpse of its role outside of time, into the dimension of space before you were born and after you will die.

God created people because He wanted a family and a relationship with that family. The Bible talks in family terms throughout: God is our *Father*, we are His *sons* and *daughters*, and fellow followers are referred to as *brothers* and *sisters*. Healthy relationship and interaction between God and humans are at the heart of why God created us. Yet, from Genesis to Revelation, the cycle we see is that God has a relationship with His children . . . they drift away . . . He works to woo them back . . . they come running back . . . He restores them . . . and the cycle starts again.

One of my favorite hymns, "Come, Thou Fount of Every Blessing," penned by Robert Robinson at age twenty-two in the year 1757, narrates this cycle so well:

O to grace how great a debtor
Daily I'm constrained to be!
Let Thy goodness, like a fetter,
Bind my wandering heart to Thee.
Prone to wander, Lord, I feel it,
Prone to leave the God I love;
Here's my heart, O take and seal it,
Seal it for Thy courts above.[6]

Yes, left to our own default setting, we are "prone to wander." Yet God is always wooing us back to Himself. He loves it when we choose to chase after Him, to pursue Him and seek Him with all our heart. If you want to step into your created purpose, seek Him with all your heart. "But if from there you seek the Lord your God, you will find him if you seek him with all your heart and with all your soul" (Deuteronomy 4:29).

The Book of Revelation gives us a glimpse of a future full of hope and destiny that also motivates our daily pursuit of prayer. Pull back the curtain of time and look at eternity. You'll be encouraged in prayer by seeing Jesus who is ever interceding for us, a great cloud of witnesses who have gone on before us cheering us on in prayer whether people named in the Bible or your relatives and loved ones, and an ongoing relationship between you and the Lord that's fostered on earth but continues eternally. Talking to God and hearing from Him during our time on earth are simply practice activities and warm-up for heaven, where we'll continue that communing relationship throughout eternity.

> **Talking to God and hearing from Him during our time on earth are simply practice activities and warm-up for heaven, where we'll continue that communing relationship throughout eternity.**

God has always planned to redeem a family for Himself from "every nation, tribe, people and language" (Revelation 7:9). This love relationship includes and is facilitated by prayer—the incredible privilege of hearing and speaking with our Father God.

God's Word tells us that prayer isn't something relegated just to life on earth. The books of Isaiah and Revelation reveal a praying church in heaven—a family all who call Him Lord will join and enjoy with Him forever. Prayer is the best work, the best use of your loving efforts. That's why one of the best gifts you could give to another is to *level the praying field* and invite them into this relationship with God.

May our first and best prayer always be: "Here's my heart, O take and seal it, seal it for Thy courts above."

Questions for Reflection

1 What intentionality to pray is in your heart going forward?

2 When you think about our life on earth being the "warm-up" time in preparation for an eternity of relationship with God, how does that expand your understanding of the value of prayer?

3 When you think of your relationship with God from His perspective, how He has always and will always long to be with you, what does that mean to you?

4 How does it impact your prayer life to realize those who have gone before you are spiritually cheering you on as Jesus is praying for you?

Notes

1. Mark Batterson, *The Circle Maker* (Grand Rapids: Zondervan, 2011) 19.

2. William W. Menzies and Stanley M. Horton, *Bible Doctrines: A Pentecostal Perspective* (Springfield, MO: Gospel Publishing House, 2012) 43–53.

3. https://www.youtube.com/watch?v=NZbQ BajYnEc (Accessed March 7, 2019).

4. www.rw360.org (Accessed March 8, 2019).

5. "Biblical Foundation for Relational Wisdom," Relational Wisdom 360, https://rw360.org/biblical-foundation-for-rw/ (Accessed March 15, 2019).

6. https://en.wikipedia.org/wiki/Come_Thou_Fount_of_Every_Blessing (Accessed March 7, 2019).

About the Author

At the age of fifteen, Donna became a follower of Christ at the altar of an Assemblies of God church in Youngstown, Ohio, Highway Tabernacle. Passionate about serving the Lord from the beginning of her Christian journey, she felt called to serve God in ministry, but her life took an unusual and circuitous path to fulfill her calling that only a sovereign God could have orchestrated.

In the late 1970s, with no examples of women in vocational ministry within view to guide or inspire her, Donna found herself in a career as a paralegal in a law office while volunteering at her church as a youth leader, youth choir director, and pioneer of a young adult ministry. Taking night classes, she graduated from Western Reserve Paralegal Institute, often wondering during those seven years working in a law office if God had forgotten about her call to ministry. All the while, she was gaining experience that would serve her well throughout ministry and ultimately fit quite nicely in her present role as general secretary of the General Council of the Assemblies of God.

The opportunity to move a step closer to ministry came in 1985, when her church hired her as bookkeeper, and she enrolled in distance learning classes for ministry through Global University's Berean School of the Bible. Having completed that training, she was licensed for ministry with the Assemblies of God in 1988 and joined the pastoral staff at Highway Tabernacle Assembly of God as youth pastor. In 1995 Parma Bethel Temple (now Parma Christian Church) near Cleveland, Ohio, invited her to serve as associate pastor overseeing Christian education, pastoral care, and missions (1995 to 2002). While there, she was ordained with the Assemblies of God (1999). That step of ordination served her well when the senior pastor of Bethel Temple retired, and the church board asked her to serve as the interim senior pastor. When the church elected a new senior pastor, Donna began exploring what would be next for her—and it turned out to be church planting.

Donna attended a church-planting training event and interviewed with her district presbytery for approval to begin this new endeavor. In October 2002, Bethel Temple released thirty-two church members and, in partnership with the Ohio Ministry Network's Church Multiplication Network, parented a new church with Donna as senior pastor: Rockside Church. Blending her experience in the business world with her love for the local church, this new assignment from God was a perfect fit for her. Located among the business professional community of Independence, a suburb known as the contemporary version of downtown Cleveland, the new church plant met in rented conference space owned by Indiana Wesleyan University. This positioned the church strategically from a financial stewardship perspective as only 4 percent of their budget went to facilities, leaving resources for 42 percent of their budget to be allocated to U.S. and World Missions. The last year Donna pastored Rockside (2017), the church was partnering with sixty-two missionaries/ missions organizations.

With a deep love for the local church and the network of churches collectively, Donna has served in leadership roles with the Assemblies of God as youth ministry representative in the 1980s, as district church planting coordinator (2004 to 2008), as district executive presbyter of the central region (2008 to 2012), and as general presbyter for Ohio (May 2014 to May 2018). Donna's unique ministry journey has been one she would never have anticipated, but one designed by God to prepare her for her current responsibility as general secretary of the Assemblies of God: the first female executive officer in the more than one-hundred-year history of the organization. In this role, her office stewards the credentials of over thirty-eight thousand ministers. Whether it's because she was a local senior pastor, a church planter, a female minister, a lifelong learner trained for ministry nontraditionally, or because she came into ministry out of the business world, Donna is an executive officer to whom many of the ministers the national office serves can personally relate.

On a personal side, she is single and enjoys her seven nieces and nephews and their children. In her spare time, she enjoys Martin guitars, biking, hiking, beach vacations, and the Cleveland Cavaliers. She currently resides in Springfield, Missouri.

For decades, Donna has been motivated by a passion for prayer, a respect for world missions, and a love for the local church. Her desire in writing this book is to inspire every person to talk to and hear from God, to encourage pastors who are equipping others for prayer, and to place tools in the hands of parents as the primary Christian educators and disciple-makers for their children—so that all may grow in their love for and connection with God through prayer.

FOR MORE INFORMATION

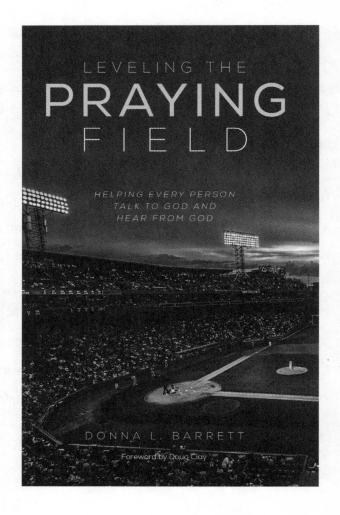

For more information about this
book and other valuable resources,
visit **www.MyHealthyChurch.com.**